American Gothic

American Gothic

Its Origins, Its Trials, Its Triumphs

Text and Photographs by Wayne Andrews

Vintage Books, A Division of Random House, New York

VINTAGE BOOKS, First Edition October 1975

Copyright © 1975 by Wayne Andrews

Originally published by Random House, Inc., New York, in 1975.

Library of Congress Cataloging in Publication Data

Andrews, Wayne. American gothic: its origin, its trials, its triumphs.

Bibliography: p. 1. Gothic revival (Architecture) — United States. 2. Architecture, Modern — 19th century —
United States.

I. Title. NA710.A53 1975b 720'.973 75-10251 ISBN 0-394-71570-5

For permission to quote from W. S. Lewis's edition of the Correspondence of Horace Walpole (1937 – 1975),
I am indebted to Yale University Press; and grateful acknowledgment is made to Little, Brown and Company, Inc.
for permission to quote from My Life in Architecture by Ralph Adams Cram.

Manufactured in the United States of America

Design and Graphics by Lidia Ferrara

Contents

Gothic
Dawn

"I have never yet seen or heard anything serious that was not ridiculous," declared Horace Walpole in 1765. Past forty-eight at the time, he was old enough to know his own mind. He has remained a disappointment to all serious-minded people, and when Macaulay came in the nineteenth century to comment on his literary career and, in particular, on his enchanting correspondence, he grew indignant. "Serious business was a trifle to him," Macaulay complained, "and trifles were his serious business . . . In everything in which Walpole busied himself, in the fine arts, in literature, in public affairs, he was drawn by some strange attraction from the great to the little, and from the useful to the odd."

But Walpole, Macaulay to the contrary, was involved in serious business. Although the pedants will never stop pointing out that he was not the first Englishman to stare with a certain admiration at the by then neglected monuments of the Middle Ages—and it must be admitted that there were antiquarians who preceded him—he may be said to have launched the Gothic revival: he made it fashionable. He was the first in the long line of conspirators who questioned the authority of the Renaissance and so laid the foundations of what we call modern architecture. Walpole might not have cared to assume this responsibility; nevertheless, but for his toy castle at Strawberry Hill we might never have witnessed the prairie-style houses of Frank Lloyd Wright, built from the inside out, or been confronted with the glass towers of Ludwig Miës van der Rohe.

A revolutionary in spite of himself, Walpole spent eighty privileged years cultivating his personal taste. Whether or not he was the son of Sir Robert Walpole, George II's redoubtable Prime Minister—gossips have hinted that Lady Walpole may have given birth to Horace after an affair with a more delicate creature than her coarse husband—he enjoyed an income that almost any other bachelor would have envied. With such an income he could afford to be impatient with bores. "They say," he murmured to a friend, "there is no English word for ennui: I think you may translate it most literally by what is called *entertaining people and doing the honors.*"

He attended Eton and King's College, Cambridge. Then, in 1739, at age twenty-two, he set off on a two-year grand tour in the company of his fellow student Thomas Gray. The two quarreled one evening, and Gray made his way back to England on his own. "The fault was mine," Walpole later confessed. "I was too young, too fond of my own diversions, nay, I do not doubt, too much intoxicated by indulgence, vanity and the insolence of my situation, as a Prime Minister's son, not to have been inattentive and insensible to the feelings of one I thought below me." They did make it up, for Walpole could not be vindictive, and Gray, shortly before he set to work on the *Elegy Written in a Country Churchyard,* was pleased to compose an ode to Walpole's cat, who had recently drowned in a tub of goldfish.

On his father's death in 1745, Walpole was left the London house on Arlington Street. There he set about nominating the men and women with whom he was to carry on his vast correspondence. Its range was wonderful, from court gossip to the quarrels of antiquarians. He was writing—and he knew it—the social history of Georgian England. Yet he never desired to pass for an author. "You know," he said, "I shun authors, and would never have been one myself, if it obliged me to keep such bad company."

To keep his own company he acquired a small country house with five acres, later extended to forty-six, at Twickenham in the London countryside. Originally built for a coachman of the Earl of Bradford and later owned by a Mrs. Chenevix, a toylady of Charing Cross, this was innocent of any architectural interest until the fall of 1749, when, at thirty-two, he determined to remodel the old house into one that would be called Strawberry Hill.

To George Montagu, whom he came to know at Eton, he gave a good hint of what he was about. Quoting from Deuteronomy, he announced: *When thou buildest a new house, then shalt thou make a battlement for thy roof, that thou bringest not blood upon thy house, if any man fall from thence.* "My house is but a sketch by beginners," he modestly claimed, but he went about it with true zeal if not true seriousness. Leaving the drudgery of the construction to one William Robinson, whom he picked up from the Board of Works, he founded a committee of taste to work with him on the project. John Chute, about to inherit The Vyne, a genuine Tudor dwelling, may be called the "architect" of Strawberry Hill, for he contributed the elevation and much else. Richard Bentley, son of the famous master at Trinity, consented to be the draftsman. As for Walpole himself, he was the antiquarian in charge, an antiquarian with a mind of his own, since he might one day summon a mason from Westminster Abbey to lay out a chapel in the woods; on another, call upon the advice of a Swiss engineer lately in the French service; and on still another, ask Robert Adam to contrive a mantelpiece.

"There is nothing I hold so cheap as a learned man," Walpole told Montagu, and the learned are likely to consider that the passion spent on Strawberry Hill was frequently misplaced. He was unafraid when Chute decided that the bookcases in the library should be copied after the side doors to the choir of old Saint Paul's, and undisturbed when Bentley came up with a mantelpiece in the little parlor that was a re-creation of the Bishop of Durham's tomb in Westminster Abbey. "Every true Goth must perceive that they [the rooms] are more the works of fancy than imitation," he argued. Which did not prevent the gallery's ceiling from echoing that of Henry VII's Chapel at Westminster.

What were friends if they could not do errands for the lord of Strawberry? "If you can pick me up any fragments of old painted glass, arms or anything, I shall be excessively obliged to you," he was writing Sir Horace Mann, the British minister at Florence, in 1750. "I can't say I remember any such thing in Italy, but out of old châteaux one might get it cheap, if there is any."

1
George Dance's portrait of
Horace Walpole at seventy-five.
Photo: National Portrait
Gallery, London.

2
Strawberry Hill (1749 – 92),
Twickenham. Designed by
Horace Walpole et al. Photo:
Wayne Andrews.

3
Gallery at Strawberry Hill
(1749 – 92), Twickenham.
Designed by Horace Walpole et
al. Photo: Wayne Andrews.

"Why will you make it Gothic?" Mann wondered. "I know it is the taste at present, but I am really sorry for it." Undiscouraged, Walpole returned to the attack. "I shall speak much more gently to you, my dear child," he went on, excusing for the moment his friend's lack of interest in the subject. "The Grecian is only proper for magnificent and public buildings. Columns and all their beautiful ornaments look ridiculous when crowded into a closet or a cheesecake house. The variety is little, and admits of no charming irregularities. I am almost as fond of the *Sharawaggi,* or Chinese want of symmetry in buildings, as in grounds and gardens. I am sure whenever you come to England, you will be pleased by the liberty of taste into which we are struck, and of which you can have no idea."

The years passed and Mann remained unconverted. "I perceive," Walpole informed him, "you have no idea what Gothic is; you have lived too long amidst true taste, to understand venerable barbarism. You say, 'you suppose my garden is to be Gothic too.' That can't be: Gothic is merely architecture, and as one has a satisfaction in imprinting the gloomth of abbeys and cathedrals on one's house, so one's garden on the contrary is to be nothing but *riant,* and the gaiety of nature."

Although Walpole did not stop improving Strawberry until 1792, by the summer of 1753 he believed that he had accomplished enough to give Sir Horace in Florence a fair account of his operations. He was proud of the lean windows fattened with rich saints in painted glass, proud of the Gothic balustrades adorned with antelopes bearing shields made of rhinoceros hides, proud of the niches full of trophies of old coats of mail and Indian shields made of rhinoceros hides, and prouder still of the broadswords, quivers, longbows, arrows and spears *supposed* to have been taken by Sir Terry Robsart in the Holy Wars.

Sir Terry, whom Walpole fancied as an ancestor, had apparently found a sure place in the family tree by the spring of 1769. "Strawberry," Montagu was informed at that time, "has been in great glory. I have given a *festino* there that will almost mortgage it. Last Tuesday all France dined there. Monsieur and Madame du Châtelet, the Duc de Liancourt . . . in short we were four and twenty. They arrived at two.

"At the gate of the castle I received them in the cravat of Gibbons' carving"—he was referring to a Grinling Gibbons woodcarving in the form of a point lace cravat that has since found its way to the Victoria and Albert Museum—"and a pair of gloves embroidered up to the elbows that had belonged to James I. The French servants stared and firmly believed this was the dress of English country gentlemen . . .

"In the evening we walked, had tea, coffee and lemonade in the gallery, which was illuminated with a thousand, or thirty candles, I forget which, and played at whist and loo until midnight. Then there was a cold supper, and at one the company returned to town saluted by fifty nightingales, who as tenants of the manor, came to do honor to their lord."

Five years before this party was given, Walpole had published *The Castle of Otranto,* the world's first Gothic novel. The genre was to become dreadfully popular in the years to come, so popular that Jane Austen could not resist a little fun on that account in *Northanger Abbey.* "Are they all horrid, are you sure they are all horrid?" asks Catherine Morland of the list of titles rattled off by her friend Isabella Thorpe. "Quite sure," comes the answer, "for a particular friend of mine, a Miss Andrews, a sweet girl, one of the sweetest creatures in the world, has read every one of them."

The typical Gothic novel — M.G. Lewis's *The Monk* comes to mind — makes so much of the horrors of the Inquisition in Latin lands that these novels must once have been required reading for all nuns with a sense of humor. But there is no mention of the Inquisition in Walpole and not even the slightest slur on the papacy. The supernatural in Gothic times was what he emphasized, whether it was the three drops of blood falling from Alfonso's statue or the enormous helmet, "a hundred times more large than any casque ever made for human being," that crashes and kills the young prince Conrad. The sable plumes atop the helmet, shivering mysteriously at angry intervals, caught in our century the attention of André Breton, the leader of the surrealists. He sensed that here was an omen worth contemplating.

Breton was also happy to find that *Otranto* could be considered an example of automatic writing. There is a letter of Walpole's that proves Breton's thesis. "I sat down and began to write, without knowing in the least what I intended to say or relate," the author told a friend. "One evening I wrote from the time I had drunk my tea, about six o'clock, till half an hour after one in the morning, when my hand and fingers were so weary, that I could not hold the pen to finish a sentence, but left Mathilda and Isabella talking in the middle of a paragraph."

The book was shyly published under the pseudonym of Onuphrio Muralto and given out as a translation of a work printed at Naples in the black letter — we might say Gothic type — in 1529. Walpole had no reason, however, to fear for the novel's success. It caught on immediately, and in the second edition he revealed that he was the author. This could have been guessed by anyone who compared the floor plan of Strawberry with that of the Italian castle.

"A frantic thing" was what Walpole called *Otranto* in his old age. "It was fit for nothing but the age in which it was written, an age . . . that required only to be amused, nor cared whether its amusements were conformable to truth and the models of good sense."

Not that he resented for a second the success he obtained by a novel inspired by his very own castle. When he traveled up and down England inspecting the various attempts to rival Strawberry Hill, he showed himself to be a kind connoisseur, scattering compliments with the grace of an ambassador. At Sir George Lyttleton's Hagley Park he was so moved by the ruined

*4
Gothic temple at Pains Hill
(c. 1750). Architect, Batty
Langley. Photo:
Wayne Andrews.
5
Gothic temple at Stowe
(c. 1739). Architect, James
Gibbs. Photo: Wayne Andrews.*

castle recently erected to the designs of Saunderson Miller that he announced that this would get its owner the "freedom even of Strawberry: it has the true rust of the Barons' Wars." And at Pains Hill, the garden of Charles Hamilton, he was also polite. "A fine place out of a most cursed hill," he decided. Here, incidentally, was a Gothic temple by Batty Langley, the author of *Gothic Architecture Improved By Rules and Proportions*, a book that had seen the light seven years before Walpole began playing architect himself. No sneer was intended; none was offered. Which might have pleased George Washington, who relied on other handbooks by Langley in building Mount Vernon.

Hagley and Pains Hill passed inspection. So did Stowe, where Lord Cobham had been so wise as to ask James Gibbs, usually remembered for that prudent church St. Martin's-in-the-Fields, to build him an awesome Gothic temple. "I adore the Gothic building," Walpole admitted, "which by some unusual inspiration Gibbs has made pure and beautiful and venerable." But his favorite was William Barrett's Lee Priory near Canterbury, the work of James Wyatt. "A child of Strawberry prettier than its parent" was his comment. Today a room from Lee Priory may be studied in the Victoria and Albert Museum.

You might suppose, since a taste for the Gothic in the eighteenth century implied that the Renaissance, respected for so long, was becoming tiresome, that Walpole would lose his temper at the sight of buildings whose creators had never strayed from the great tradition. This was not the case. Although he did cry out, in a cross moment, that Louis XIV's garden at Versailles was something for "a great child," he was a tolerant visitor to estates more conventional than his own. When he came to Lord Westmoreland's Mereworth Castle, one of the greater Palladian villas, he found it "so perfect in a Palladian taste that I must own it has recovered me a little from Gothic." One reason may have been that its architect Colen Campbell had also designed Houghton Hall in Norfolk, the seat of Sir Robert Walpole. Horace worshiped his father's memory, and the saddest moments of his life were those in which he contemplated the fate of Houghton, gone to shambles in the hands of an improvident nephew. "You and I," he wrote Sir Horace Mann as the American Revolution was coming to its end, "have lived long enough to see Houghton and England emerge, the one from a country gentleman's house to a palace, the other, from an island to an empire; and to behold both stripped of their acquisitions and lamentable in their ruins."

The lord of Strawberry always spoke his own mind, and his literary judgments will appall professors who believe that English literature may safely be taught in our universities. He knew that Dr. Johnson was "an ill-natured bear, and in opinions as senseless a bigot as an old washerwoman." He also knew that *Tristram Shandy* was "a very insipid and tedious performance."

So it was altogether natural that his closest confidante was Madame du Deffand, the blind but sure Frenchwoman he sought out again and again in

Paris. Like Walpole, she stood for no nonsense, and did not hesitate to tell her old friend Voltaire to "lay off those priests." She seems to have hoped for a closer friendship than would have suited Walpole. "You are magnificent when it comes to the hors-d'oeuvre," she reminded him.

Walpole did not welcome the French Revolution. He had met the *philosophes* in Paris and they bored him. "Freethinking is for oneself, surely not for society," he believed. The American Revolution was something else. "The next Augustan age will dawn on the other side of the Atlantic," he assured Sir Horace Mann not long after the First Continental Congress assembled in Philadelphia.

He died, having inherited his father's earldom of Orford, on the second of March 1791. "My buildings are paper, like my writings," he once said, "and both will be blown away in ten years after I am dead." This was not true. Strawberry Hill is still here, safe in the hands of Saint Mary's College of the Congregation of Saint Paul, which has repaired the damage done by a fire bomb in the last world war. As for the writings, the Yale edition of his correspondence under the editorship of Wilmarth S. Lewis has already reached its thirty-ninth volume.

A generation would pass before the United States made the attempt to become a medieval nation, but there was a sign in Walpole's lifetime that his message was understood. We know that in 1771 Thomas Jefferson thought of ornamenting a mountaintop near Monticello with a battlemented tower, and that he planned, if he did not actually erect, "a small Gothic temple of antique appearance" to distinguish the graveyard of his family and servants.

Such was the beginning of *American Gothic.*

Gothic
Morning

He was an actor, not a gentleman, reported the painter Henry Fuseli. But there were others who recognized that William Beckford's Gothic ambition was unforgettable, no matter what impression he made on the polite public. Horace Walpole's friend George Selwyn, who met him one evening in 1782, admitted that "he seems to possess very extraordinary talents; he is a perfect master of music, but has a voice, either natural or feigned, of an eunuch. He speaks several languages with uncommon facility, but he has such a mercurial turn that I think he may finish his days *aux petites maisons*." Walpole himself, who may or may not have heard that Beckford dismissed Strawberry Hill as a "Gothic mousetrap," seems to have shared his friend's fear that here was a man who would die mad. Yet Walpole may have detected in this instance how much taste was buried under so much arrogance. He referred to him as "the alderman's son, who has just enough parts to lead him astray from common sense."

The first Beckford of whom anyone has heard was a slop seller in seventeenth-century London. During the reign of Charles II, his brother went off to Jamaica, where his son, who became governor of the island, died in 1711, worth more than half a million pounds. The governor's grandson, educated at Westminster in England, rose to be not only alderman of London's Billingsgate Ward but also lord mayor, leaving on his death in 1770 what was presumed to be the most colossal fortune in England, much of which was invested in sugar plantations and slaves. This source of income did not prevent him from becoming the savage champion of the radical John Wilkes. On the night Wilkes was released from prison, the word LIBERTY in white letters three feet high was emblazoned on the Beckford town house in Soho. "Luckily, the evening was wet," Horace Walpole commented, "and not a mouse was stirring."

William Beckford was the only child of the lord mayor and his wife, the former Maria Hamilton, granddaughter of the sixth Earl of Abercorn. She never learned to control her temper—neither did her son—and she could not have been a good mother to young William, left fatherless at ten. Yet every precaution was taken to give the child a perfect or perhaps too perfect an education. His godfather, William Pitt, seems to have raised no objection when he was not sent away to school but placed in the hands of tutors. He learned French as soon as he learned English, and he picked up the elements of architecture from Sir William Chambers, the creator of Somerset House. What he knew of painting came from Alexander Cozens, the talented watercolorist who had been a drawing master at Eton and who did nothing to scotch the rumor that he was the illegitimate son of Peter the Great. There is also the legend that Mozart, when eight, was brought to the Beckford mansion to teach the four-year-old heir his five-finger exercises. This may have been true. "We renewed our acquaintance in Vienna," Beckford revealed, "where I found him as strange, as melancholy, but more wonderful than ever."

At seventeen Beckford was off to Geneva, surely not to improve his French, which needed no improving: he and the Anthony Hamilton of his mother's family who left us the *Mémoires du Comte de Gramont*, are the only two Englishmen to meet French standards in French prose. To Beckford English standards were tiresome. "To glory in horses, to know how to knock up and cure them, to smell of the stable, swear, talk bawdy, eat roast beef, drink, speak bad French, go to Lyons and come back again with manly disorders are qualifications not despicable in the eyes of the English here," he wrote Cozens from Geneva in the fall of 1777. "Such an animal I am determined not to be!"

He was back in England and nearly nineteen when he called at Powderham Castle near Exeter, the seat of the Courtenays. There he came upon William Courtenay, a boy of eleven with long curls and languid eyes who had grown up with twelve sisters. "It is a sad thing that I cannot see you every day and every hour," he wrote young Courtenay about this time, "since you are the only person (yes let me repeat it once more) to whom I can communicate my feelings—or to whom I can disclose the strange wayward passion which throbs this very instant in my bosom."

The passion did not escape the notice of the Beckford family. To give him something else to think about, they invited Peter Beckford, William's first cousin, a forty-year-old fox hunter, and his twenty-five-year-old wife, the former Louisa Pitt, down to Fonthill in Wiltshire, the old mayor's country house, which had recently been enlarged by Sir John Soane. Louisa fell in love with William, that is obvious. And it is also obvious that she realized how much "Kitty"—so they named William Courtenay—meant to him. "How my heart bounds with transport when I fancy that after Kitty I am the being you prefer to all others," Louisa would one day write him.

The family fancied that a grand tour might divert Beckford, and in June 1780 he was off to the Germanys and finally to Naples, where he could not avoid calling on Sir William Hamilton, the British minister who happened to be his mother's cousin. Lady Hamilton, a deeply religious woman with a rare talent at the harpsichord, was not so lenient as Louisa Beckford, but did take pity on her visitor. "You have taken the first steps," she pleaded with him, "continue to resist and every day you will find the struggle less—the *important* struggle—what is it for? no less than *honor*, *reputation*, and all that an honest and noble soul holds dear, while infamy, *eternal infamy* (my Soul freezes when I write the word) attends the giving way to the soft alluring of a criminal passion."

Beckford may have listened to her advice; we know that he heard her on the harpsichord. "Music destroys me," he told her, "and what is worse, I love being destroyed." This was rhetoric. So, we suppose, was his final comment on Lady Hamilton at the keyboard: "No performer that I ever heard produced such soothing effects; they seemed the emanations of a pure, uncontaminated mind."

Music was not forgotten at the coming-of-age party he gave at Fonthill in the fall of 1781. The great castrato Pacchierotti—whom Beckford had heard at Lucca in his favorite opera, Bertoni's *Quinto Fabio*—starred in *Il Tributo*, a pastoral cantata by Rauzzini, but this was only one of the treats in store for the ten or twelve thousand people who poured through the gates of the family estate. Three hundred guests sat down to dinner in Fonthill's Grecian Hall, and bonfires on the downs and rockets exploding while colored lights picked out the architectural details confirmed the fact that Beckford was rich. It was said that his capital ran to a million pounds, from which he derived an income of a hundred thousand pounds a year.

Louisa Beckford was on hand. So was William Courtenay. They were also on hand at Christmastime, when the Alsatian painter Philip James de Loutherbourg, a friend of Cagliostro's who had made good in London designing stage sets for David Garrick, was hired to bathe the family mansion in "a delicate roseate glow." Pacchierotti sang again, joined by his fellow castrati Tenducci and Rauzzini, and Beckford was more than pleased. Fifty-seven years later he wrote: "I still feel warmed and irradiated by the recollections of that strange, necromantic light which Loutherbourg had thrown over what absolutely appeared a realm of Fairy, or rather, perhaps, a Demon Temple deep beneath the earth set apart for tremendous mysteries—and yet, how soft, how genial was this quiet light."

Loutherbourg did his work so well that before the spring had passed, Beckford completed *Vathek*, the Oriental tale in which Louisa may be said to play the role of Nouronihar and William Courtenay that of Gulchenrouz. "I wrote *Vathek* when I was twenty-two years old," he boasted. "I wrote it at one sitting and in French. It cost me three days and two nights of hard labor." He did not labor in vain, for Stéphane Mallarmé, while recognizing that this was the work of a cautious foreigner who could not take too many liberties with the language, congratulated him on reaching the perfection of Voltaire, and what was even more amazing, prophesying the coming of Chateaubriand.

We may be sure that Beckford was in ecstasy during the Christmas party at Fonthill, but we may never know what actually went on. There were ugly rumors. "The Begum"—this was Beckford's nickname for his mother—"is raving at a rate the prince of the abyss himself has no conception of," he wrote Louisa. "*All* the wild tales which were so charitably circulated of our orientalism . . . Be not alarmed, Louisa. Let us defy their venom. The more it rankles—the more your soul will be rivetted to mine."

A flight to the Continent was not only desirable, it was inevitable, and the gossip did not come to an end when in the spring of 1783, he married Lady Margaret Gordon, daughter of the fourth Earl of Aboyne. They found it convenient to escape to Switzerland and France. Living even in retirement at Fonthill was impossible. She was to die in the spring of 1786, shortly after giving birth to their second daughter, who eventually became the Duchess of

6
"I grow rich," said Beckford,
"and mean to build towers."
Fonthill Abbey (1796 – 1807).
Architect, James Wyatt. From
Rutter's Delineations of
Fonthill, 1823. Photo: Avery
Library, Columbia University.
7
Staircase, Fonthill Abbey
(1796 – 1807). Architect, James
Wyatt. From Rutter's
Delineations of Fonthill,
1823. Photo: Avery Library,
Columbia University.

Hamilton.* To the end Lady Margaret was loyal to her husband. "I was not to abandon a man," she insisted, "who had always behaved to me with the greatest tenderness and affection."

The persecution, however, was eternal. He fled to Portugal in 1787, only to find that the British minister, Sir Robert Walpole—a cousin of Horace's—not only refused to meet him and warned the English colony against him, but also made it impossible for him to be received by the Queen, Maria I. She was mentally deranged at the time, and Beckford's only consolation was that he was near her one day—he was only a room or two distant, and could hear her agonizing shrieks, which, he said, "inflicted upon me a sensation of horror such as I never felt before."

When he traveled, he brought along his own piano, his own wines and the pick of his eighty-seven servants, but the reputation he had earned remained a burden, and the memory of William Courtenay was no comfort. "That effeminate fool!" he called him. "I have been hunted down and persecuted these many years. I have been stung and not allowed opportunities of changing the snarling, barking style . . . I sigh for the pestilential breath of an African serpent to destroy every Englishman who comes in my way."

There was a time, in 1797, when he imagined he could redeem himself by being sent to Paris to bring about peace with the Directory, but nothing came of this, and by the summer of 1799 he returned to the solitude of his father's mansion in Wiltshire. Fonthill, he decided, must be pulled down, and in its place a Gothic castle should rise that would dwarf not only that Gothic temple at his uncle Charles Hamilton's Pains Hill, but "that old imbecile Walpole's gimcrack villa."

His architect was James Wyatt, the very man whose Lee Priory had pleased the builder of Strawberry. He was talented, but difficult. "If Wyatt can get near a large fire and have a bottle by him, he cares for nothing else," Beckford noticed. The first plans dated from 1796; not until 1807 was Fonthill Abbey completed and the last of Mayor Beckford's belongings auctioned off. The owner was easily exasperated, and we may imagine his rage when the great tower crashed in 1799. For once he controlled himself. "We shall," he said, "rise again more gloriously than ever, provided the sublime Wyatt will graciously deign to bestow a little more commonplace attention upon what I supposed to be his favorite structure." In the meantime he erected a wall to banish the public. "They will take no denial when they go hunting in their red jackets to excruciate to death a poor hare," he railed against his neighbors. "I found remonstrances vain, and so I built the wall to exclude them."

Convenience was not his aim, but, as Byron put it in *Don Juan*, Gothic daring shown in English money. Although there were eighteen bedrooms, thirteen of these, thanks to their almost inaccessible height, their smallness and

*She was the great-great-grandmother of the Duke of Hamilton, to whose estate the Nazi Rudolf Hess flew in the spring of 1941.

their want of light or ventilation, were virtually unusable, and the lord of the Abbey was reduced to sleeping in the chintz boudoir on the second floor. This, too, was hardly comfortable. Grandeur, however, was evident. The great tower was one hundred and forty-five feet high, the gallery was one hundred and eighty-five feet long, and the chapel for the Blessed Saint Anthony—Lisbon's patron saint and apparently Beckford's as well—was seventy-two feet high and sixty-six feet wide.

Toward the end of 1800, five hundred workmen were employed day and night, torches and lamps being brought into play to honor Beckford's impatience. And on December 20, Lord Nelson arrived, the hero of the Battle of the Nile, accompanied by Sir William Hamilton and the Emma who replaced the Lady Hamilton Beckford had known twenty years ago. Emma, once a prostitute and later the mistress of Sir William's nephew, may have known nothing about the Greek and Etruscan vases her husband had been collecting for so long in Naples, but she was aware, even though she had gained weight, that this was the perfect time to exhibit one of her "attitudes" before Lord Nelson, the latest of her lovers. On the twenty-third, the final night of the festivities, once the company sat down to dinner, she gave her famous representation of Agrippina, Nero's mother, bearing the ashes of her father, Germanicus. "The action of her head, of her hands and arms," remarked one spectator, "was most classically graceful," and "her action . . . so just and natural . . . as to draw tears from several of the company."

But Beckford himself may have put on the best show of all. On Emma's night the staircases were lighted "by certain mysterious living figures at different intervals, dressed in hooded gowns, and standing with large wax torches in their hands." One of those who admired this performance was Benjamin West, the American who had become George III's favorite painter.

"The tower sings a fine tune," Beckford was writing two years later to Sir William Hamilton, "and all the little turrets, flying buttresses, pinnacles and Gothic loopholes join in the chorus." He may have been momentarily encouraged by the visit of Lord Nelson, but the cloud over his reputation remained. Although Turner dared to make three watercolor sketches of Fonthill Abbey, crossing Beckford's threshold was likely to prove an embarrassment. The Bishop of Salisbury considered paying a call, but was stopped in time by the gentlemen of the country. And Sir Richard Colt-Hoare, anxious to compare Fonthill with his own domain at Stourhead, lived to regret the hours he spent with Beckford. Called to account by his fellow magistrates, he was forced to explain that his visit was "for purposes of information," no more. "What a damned fool I was to let him in at all!" his host commented.

In the end Beckford grew bored. He made more than one alteration, then in 1813, when Wyatt died, lost interest. In 1822 he gave out that the Abbey and its contents would be put up for auction. Christie's sold 72,000 copies of the catalog, but a week or two before the sale was to take place, it was announced that the house and grounds, with the contents, had been sold to a certain John Farquhar, who had made his money selling gunpowder to the East India Company. The price was £330,000, or £63,000 more than Beckford had spent on the project.

At Bath, where he moved to Lansdown Crescent and built a tower one hundred and twenty feet high crowned with a cast-iron reproduction of the choragic monument of Lysicrates at Athens, he enjoyed the view before him. "This! This!" he said, "the finest prospect in Europe." His enjoyment of this view was interrupted one day when he was summoned to attend the bedside of a dying man. The man was the clerk of the works at Fonthill, who reported to him that the arch of the tower was unsafe. Beckford related this news to the new owner, who declared that the "tower would last his time." It didn't. Fonthill Abbey collapsed into a ruin on the twenty-first of December 1825.

The ruin would have pleased Lord Byron, who died the year before. When he set out for Greece in 1823, he carried a copy of *Vathek* in his luggage, and he mentioned Beckford's Portuguese villa in *Childe Harold*. The two never met, although Byron tried to reach him. "To what good would it have led?" Beckford asked. "We should have both met in full drill—both endeavored to have been delighted—a correspondence would have been established, the most laborious that can be imagined, because the most artificial."

The last discovery Beckford made was of Benjamin Disraeli's prose. "How wildly original! How full of intense thought! How awakening!" he exclaimed on reading Disraeli's novel *Contarini Fleming*. They met only once, at the opera in the summer of 1834. Beckford was "very bitter and *malin*," Disraeli wrote down in his notebook, "but full of warm feelings for the worthy." Yes, but not too warm. "I am surprised that he has not a better French accent," Beckford observed on listening to the report of an agent who had looked Dizzy up in London. This was sad. Sad, too, was the fact that Disraeli was found smoking with his father and brother in the family sitting room.

In 1843, the year of Dicken's *Christmas Carol*, Beckford had already thoughts of his own about how to celebrate Christmas. "Stupid family parties, mercilessly fatted meat, foul sausages, worn out sermons, every possible excuse for gourmandizing and praying to no purpose are the characteristics of this present season, from which really wholesome animal food and sound spiritual doctrine are equally banished. This *wretched farce* will be superseded ere long by a *frightful tragedy*." He wrote this on Christmas Day.

He prepared his own tomb at Lansdown Crescent, visited it daily and looked after the flowers. When he died, in his eighty-fourth year, on May 2, 1844, he left instructions that two lines he had written thirty years before at Fonthill should be set on his grave. They read:

Eternal Power!
Grant me through obvious clouds one transient gleam
Of thy bright essence in my dying hour!

By this time the Gothic gesture that Walpole invented and Beckford did so much to advertise had spread far beyond England. As early as 1787 Bazhenov and Kazakof had begun Tsaritsyno, a Gothic palace in the environs of Moscow. This did not please Catherine, and Tsaritsyno is today a splendid ruin. Seven years after Bazhenov and Kazakov were at work, a certain Brendel, a carpenter from Potsdam, laid the first stone for a glorious fake Gothic ruin on Peacock Island in Berlin. The sight charmed the House of Hohenzollern, and by 1826 the great architect Schinkel built a Gothic *Kavalierhaus* nearby, on whose lawn, in 1852, the famous Rachel recited a scene from Racine's *Athalie* for the benefit of Frederick William IV.

This was stage scenery, all of it, and so was Sedgeley, the first Gothic house in the United States, designed by Benjamin Henry Latrobe in 1799 for William Crammond of Philadelphia, a gentleman with an interest in rolling mills. Latrobe, however, was a serious architect, the man to whom we owe most of what is best in the Capitol at Washington.

And the Gothic Revival in the nineteenth century was to become a serious matter.

8
Gothic ruin on Peacock
Island, Berlin (1794–97).
Architect, Brendel. Photo:
Wayne Andrews.

9
Kavalierhaus (1826), on
Peacock Island, Berlin.
Architect, Karl Friedrich
Schinkel. Photo:
Wayne Andrews.

10
Sedgeley (1799), residence of
William Crammond,
Philadelphia, Pennsylvania;
demolished. Architect, Benjamin
Henry Latrobe. From William
Birch's The Country Seats of
the United States of North
America, 1808. Photo: New
York-Historical Society.

11
Tsaritsyno (1787), near
Moscow. Architects, Bazhenov
and Kazakof. Photo:
Wayne Andrews.

Augustus Welby Northmore Pugin was one of the saints of the Gothic Revival, the first to take the Gothic in dead earnest, and the first to discover that the architecture of the Renaissance was infamous.

His father, a Frenchman who came from no one knows where and may have been a friend at one time of the revolutionary painter David, reached London as a refugee from the Revolution, wearing a three-cornered hat and carrying a gold-headed cane. He found a job in the office of John Nash, then cheerfully designing a number of Gothic castles, and graciously consented to perfect Nash's knowledge of Gothic details. He also married a Miss Catherine Welby, the daughter of a barrister. She was an indignant woman who doted on the indignant sermons of a certain Edward Irving, a Scotsman, the founder in London of a sect of his own. His sermons, which usually ran to three hours—he could on occasion, bring himself down to an hour and forty minutes—did not please young Pugin. "There are many paths leading into the Road to Rome," one of his perceptive biographers had written. "*Disgust* is the name of one of them."

He was an only child, born on the first of March 1812, in time to benefit from the discipline his mother imposed on his father's articled students. She went to bed at nine and rose at four. At six she expected the students to get to work. This regime did not prevent Pugin from leading his life in his own way. At nineteen he became a scene painter in charge of all the sets for *Kenilworth*, the production staged by the Italian Opera Company, and he was only fifteen when he began designing Gothic furniture for Windsor Castle. Later on, he was merciless toward his achievements as a cabinetmaker. "A man who remains any length of time in a modern Gothic room and escapes without being wounded by some of its minutiae, may consider himself extremely fortunate," he wrote. "There are often as many pinnacles and gablets about a pier-glass frame as are to be found in an ordinary church, and not infrequently the whole canopy of a tomb has been transferred for the purpose, as at Strawberry Hill." He himself perpetrated "many of these enormities."

No one could turn out Gothic ornaments with quite the skill of the team of workmen he set up in his office, but this business brought him to bankruptcy. In its way this was a blessing: he became an architect on his own, responsible for a hundred-odd churches.

There seems to be some doubt about the exact date on which he was received into the Roman Catholic Church. Was the ornamentalist turned architect twenty-two or twenty-three? But there is no doubt that "received" is too tame a word to describe his conversion. He was to adore the Church of Rome with all the fervor he lavished on Gothic architecture, and he was a Goth who never knew the meaning of moderation. "Milk-and-water men never effect anything," he pronounced "They deserve drowning in their own insipid compositions."

When he acknowledged "a most acceptable and kind present . . . in the shape of an enormous Cheddar cheese," he pointed out that "although not strictly Gothic in its present shape," it could "daily be rendered more so by cutting it into four, which will make it a quatrefoil." And his joy in his third wife, the first two having died, may be measured when he described her as "a first-rate Gothic woman at last, who perfectly understands and delights in spires, chancels, screens, stained windows, brasses and vestments."

The Roman Church that he worshiped must, he insisted, do away with all the pagan trappings introduced during the Renaissance. These he came to loathe with a violence that must have surprised Romans baptized at birth. "A man may be judged," he proclaimed, "by his feelings on Plain Chaunt. If he likes Mozart, he is no chancel and screen man."

As for Alberti and the other masters of the Renaissance, who had taught the world that great architecture consisted in the principle of symmetry and in the perfection of proportions, they were so many traitors. His strong feelings on this subject may have alarmed John Talbot, the sixteenth Earl of Shrewsbury and Waterford. This devout Roman was his most generous patron, calling on him to make additions and alterations to Alton Towers, the family's Gothic castle in Staffordshire, and footing the bills for St. Mary's, Uttoxeter, St. Chad's, Birmingham and many another church.

"Happily," wrote Pugin in the later days of his conversion, "at that time I did not cross the Alps, so I escaped the severest of all trials for the faith of the neophyte—the Eternal City." When he did get to Rome he was so annoyed that he considered leaving town without seeing the Pope. The cupola of St. Peter's was "a humbug, a failure, an abortion, a mass of imposition and a sham constructed even more vilely than it was designed." But, as he told Lord Shrewsbury, "I do not despair of St. Peter's being rebuilt in a better style. I saw two prelates at Rome in immediate attendance on the Pope, who quite agreed with me. What absurdities people have talked and written about the pointed style not being adapted for Italy! Why, it is full of it; there is not a little town that does not contain some fine specimens, to my astonishment."

What Pugin did was considerable. There were those hundred churches in England and Ireland for his fellow Romans. There was Scarisbrick Hall in Lancashire, the princely mansion of the bachelor Charles Scarisbrick, said to be the richest commoner in England. And there were the Houses of Parliament; when Sir Charles Barry undertook this commission after the fire of 1834, he prevailed upon Pugin to provide the ornamental details. "Barry is the right man in the right place," Pugin gratefully acknowledged. "What more could we wish?" Which meant that he appreciated his chance at Barry's side even if he did fret at times over contriving things like "eighteen umbrella stands of quaint design."

What Pugin dared was even more remarkable. In the books and pamphlets he published, he proposed turning the nineteenth century upside down: the modern world could be saved from damnation only by the Roman Catholic

12
Scarisbrick Hall (1837 – 60).
Designed by A. W. N. Pugin and
completed, with tower, by his son
after his death. Photo:
Wayne Andrews.

faith and the Catholic architecture of the Middle Ages. "Everything glorious about the English churches is Catholic, everything debased and hideous, Protestant," he declared in *Contrasts: Or a Parallel between Noble Edifices of the Middle Ages and Corresponding Buildings of the Present Day: Shewing the Present Decay of Taste*, the first edition of which he brought out in 1836.

He was no common scold. "The author," he argued, "is quite ready to maintain the principle of contrasting Catholic excellence with modern degeneracy; and wherever that degeneracy is observable, be it in Protestant or Catholic countries, it will be found to proceed from the decay of true Catholic principles and practice." So that no one could miss the point, he included a sketch of a Catholic town of 1440 and the very same town in 1840.

"It is now, indeed, time," he proclaimed, "to break the chains of paganism which have enslaved the Christians of the last three centuries." He realized that "before true taste and Christian feelings can be revived, all the present and popular ideas on the subject must be utterly changed." He looked forward to the day when the "*famous edifices* of modern Europe" would "sink into masses of deformity by the side of the neglected and mouldering piles of Catholic antiquity."

This angry man could also be strangely rational: he was the first of the Gothic revivalists to talk common sense. "The great test of architectural beauty is the fitness of the design to the purpose for which it is intended," he believed. "The style of a building should so correspond with its use that the spectator may at once perceive the purpose for which it was erected."

He was aware that he was living in a chaotic age. "Private judgment runs riot," he complained in *An Apology for the Revival of Christian Architecture* that he brought out in 1843. "Every architect has a theory of his own, a *beau idéal* he has himself created, a disguise with which to invest the building he erects. This is generally the result of his latest travels. One breathes nothing but the Alhambra—another the Parthenon—a third is full of lotus cups and pyramids from the banks of the Nile—a fourth, from Rome, is all dome and basilica." And he came to the conclusion that "styles are now *adapted* instead of *generated*, and ornament and design *adapted to*, instead of *generated by*, the edifices themselves."

There were days when he despaired of the proper response from the Romans. "Do not deceive yourself," he wrote a Roman who could comprehend him, "the Catholics will cut their own throats, the clergy will put down religion . . . We have a detestable crew to deal with—ignorance, prejudice, timidity, tepidity. . . . Actually, Protestants are far better inclined to Catholicism than half the soi-disant Catholics of our days."

His only refuge from his troubles was to escape on his yacht. "There is nothing worth living for but Christian architecture and a boat," he explained, but this refuge was to fail him. In the summer of 1852 he perplexed a friend by breaking the news of a dreadful calamity in the harbor. Five ships, he said,

13
Church of St. James the Less
(1846 – 48), Philadelphia,
Pennsylvania. Architects, Place
& Carner. Photo:
Wayne Andrews.

had sunk while trying to clear the entrance. No such disaster had occurred, and Pugin, after being placed under the proper restraint, was shortly afterward removed to Bedlam. He died at forty in his own home on September 14, 1852. At the very end he enjoyed the delusion that all churches had become one, and he began making out imaginary checks to clergymen for the benefit of the poor.

His message was appreciated in England, and not only by the Romans. As early as 1836, what became the Cambridge Camden Society was founded at Trinity College at Cambridge by undergraduates who shared Pugin's love of medieval art, and were as anxious as he could have desired to reform church ceremonies and restore and preserve the early churches. They also had earnest ideas about what type of churches should be built in their own time: in November 1841 they began publishing the *Ecclesiologist* to spread the word. They even succeeded in dictating the design of one American church, St. James the Less in Philadelphia, erected in 1846 - 48 to plans provided by a certain G. G. Place in England and carried out by the Philadelphia architect John E. Carver.

But America was no longer a British colony, and the Gothic revival in America went its own way, no matter if its English origin could never be forgotten. The Gothic remained a stage set in the early years of the nineteenth century, as you could tell by glancing at the Chapel of St. Mary's Seminary in Baltimore, built for the Sulpicians in 1807 by the French refugee Maximilien Godefroy. This church exhibited a barrel vault over which Pugin, with his knowledge of Gothic vaulting, might have frowned. And the Gothic of Strawberry Hill was doubtless in the mind of the carpenters who worked c. 1812 on the quaint clubhouse at Eddington, Pennsylvania, of the Castle of the State in Schuylkill. Strawberry must also have haunted Daniel Wadsworth, later the patron of Thomas Cole, when he began building Montevideo, his seat at Avon near Hartford, Connecticut, toward 1818. This was a mere frame structure, and it is strange that its crenelated rooftop has not yet been washed away in a thunderstorm.

To Wadsworth, gloom was a wonderful and natural attribute of the Gothic. Yet, as he admitted in a lecture to a young ladies' seminary, "there is nothing in the mere forms or embellishments of the pointed style. . . in the least adapted to convey to the mind the impression of *Gothic Gloom*." Perhaps, he suggested, this charm was due to the venerable age and shrouded windows of a building like Westminster Abbey.

Congressman Gulian C. Verplanck of New York, the tried and true friend of Washington Allston—the only American painter with a Gothic novel to his credit—dismissed gloom from consideration when he delivered an address on architecture in the spring of 1824 before the American Academy of the Fine Arts. Instead, paraphrasing Sir Joshua Reynolds' *Thirteenth Discourse,* he made much of the "peculiar and deeply interesting associations" of Gothic

14
St. Mary's Chapel (1807),
Baltimore, Maryland. Architect,
Maximilien Godefroy. Photo:
Wayne Andrews.

buildings, "which, I know not how, throw back the architectural remains of the Middle Ages to a much remoter antiquity in the imagination than those of Rome and Athens."

Verplanck had hit upon the essence of the Gothic message for Americans in the years from Jackson to Lincoln: the builder of a Gothic mansion could live in a Gothic time, and the fourth dimension, time itself, became one of the aims of any architect who tried to reach the American public. No one was more aware of this than Andrew Jackson Downing, the landscape gardener from Newburgh, New York, who did more than anyone else to make sure that the United States would be a medieval nation. Downing was clever, preaching make-believe one day, and on the next, imposing upon his vast audience verities that Frank Lloyd Wright would have been happy to claim as his own.

He warned Americans against big houses, foreseeing that the pride and joy of today might be the white elephant of tomorrow. He also emphasized, in language very like Wright's, the importance of expressing the nature of materials. "When we employ stone," he pleaded, "let it be clearly expressed; when we employ wood, there should be no less frankness in avowing the material." Faking was not desirable. "We could point," he added, "to two or three of these imitations of Gothic castles, with towers and battlements built of wood. Nothing can well be more paltry and contemptible. The sugar castles of confectioners and pastry cooks are far more admirable as works of art." This advice was frequently disregarded, but it was offered nonetheless.

And if Downing did not have the occasion to say, as did Wright, that Taliesin would not be *on* the hill at Spring Green, Wisconsin, but *of* the hill, he understood very well what Wright would one day be about in planning his domain: the site was to be studied before the first sketch was made of any house. "The castellated style," Downing insisted, "never appears completely at home except in wild and romantic scenery, or in situations where the neighboring mountains, or wild passes, are sufficiently near to give that character to the landscape. In such localities the Gothic castle affects us agreeably, because we know that baronial castles were generally built in similar spots."

Timid men, Downing made plain, should never dream of building houses with "steep gables, unsymmetrical and capricious forms." He added, "There is something wonderfully captivating in the idea of a battlemented castle, even to an apparently modest man, who thus shows to the world his unsuspected vein of personal ambition, by trying to make a castle of his country house. But, *unless there is something of the castle in the man,* it is very likely, if it be like a real castle, to dwarf him to the stature of a mouse."

He dismissed as ridiculous the slur that his message was un-American. "It is," he said, "as absurd for the critics to ask for the *American style* of architecture as it was for the English friends of a Yankee of our acquaintance to request him to do them the favor to put on his savage dress and talk a little

15
Montevideo (c. 1818), residence
of Daniel Wadsworth, who
designed it, Avon, Connecticut.
Photo: Wayne Andrews.

16
Highland Garden (c. 1841),
residence of Andrew Jackson
Downing, Newburgh, New
York; demolished. (Whether
Downing was the architect of his
own house remains a question.)
From Downing's Treatise, New
York, 1860. Photo: Nemo Warr.

American . . . No original style ever existed" — of that he was sure — "All were modifications."

"The finest whispers of nature thrilled his frame like a well-tuned harp," wrote one of Downing's admirers when he died in 1852 at thirty-seven, the hero of a steamboat disaster on the Hudson. He could be charming, as all visitors to Highland Garden, the Gothic villa he built for himself at Newburgh, would testify. There were magnolias to be found on the breakfast plates of favored guests, and he took care, as a gentleman should, that no sign of toil could be discovered in his home — no sign, that is, except the pile of letters he had yet to answer on his writing table.

He did labor. The campaign for Central Park, for which he fought at the side of William Cullen Bryant, devoured much of his time. He also wrote one book after another. His first success, *A Treatise on the Theory and Practice of Landscape Gardening*, brought out in 1841, was followed by *Cottage Residences*, *Rural Essays* and the *Architecture of Country Houses*. He also had a magazine of his own, *The Horticulturalist*. With this organ at his disposal, he did not hesitate to put the Greek revival, which he detested, in its place. Like the Gothic revival, it had been imported in 1799 by Latrobe, and was flourishing in Downing's lifetime. He hoped and believed it was dying. "The Greek temple disease has passed its crisis," he reported in 1846. "The people have survived it."

He was lucky to find an architect whom he could trust. Not blindly, for Alexander Jackson Davis, whom he promoted everywhere, and whose drawings illustrated his books, was guilty of more than one specimen in the Grecian style. But Davis — Downing realized this — was a Goth at heart. He was bound to be his ally, no matter if "slang articles" about him appeared now and then in magazines that Downing did not edit.

The most successful architect of his generation, and one of the most successful in American history, Davis was a dedicated romantic, a man who never outgrew his childhood taste for Gothic novels. He seems to have experienced no financial crises. Retiring from the profession in his sixties, he died at eighty-nine in the comfort of a Gothic cottage of his own design at Llewellyn Park, the fashionable subdivision in West Orange, New Jersey, laid out for the wholesale druggist Llewellyn Haskell.

Davis was a superb draftsman, and it is easy to understand the surprise and delight with which painters the like of Rembrandt Peale and John Trumbull gazed at his first sketches. He also knew the art of conquering clients: he could talk a Southern general into a Gothic mansion as easily as he could a leather merchant in Bridgeport, Connecticut. Nor did he neglect the details of his business. Well aware that every customer could not afford to have him supervise designs, he worked up a handsome mail-order trade in plans that could be carried out by local carpenters. One example of the mail-order Davis is the charming Gothic cottage at Rhinebeck on the Hudson, done to please the town banker Henry Delamater.

17
Residence (1844) of Henry
Delamater, Rhinebeck, New
York. Architect, Alexander
Jackson Davis. Photo:
Wayne Andrews.

Although the son of the editor of a Congregational review, Davis, if we may judge by the diaries he left behind, never chose to be serious-minded. In 1820, at seventeen, he set down in so many words his philosophy. "I do not intend to trouble myself much about what business to follow as a livelihood, but jog along through the world without cares and at my ease," he informed a favorite aunt. "It's the best way." It may not have been the best way for Davis's wife, who devoted a quarter of a century to the board of managers of the Women's Prison Association of New York. She may not have come along when he visited the artists and writers he chose for his friends. He was fond of calling at Thomas Cole's studio at Catskill and enjoyed more than one stroll with Elihu Vedder, the painter of "The Lost Mind." He would also go hiking with Herman Melville in the Berkshires, or talk away an afternoon in town with Fenimore Cooper or the Southern novelist William Gilmore Simms.

Davis got his chance in 1829, when Ithiel Town, a bridge builder with a rich architectural library, asked him into his New York office as his partner. Town was off to Europe before the year was over, leaving Davis in charge, and the partnership was terminated in 1835, to be resumed, briefly, in 1842–43. Although Town collaborated on the Gothic hall of New York University on Washington Square—lovingly recalled by S. F. B. Morse in an allegorical landscape—and again on the Gothic Wadsworth Museum with which Daniel Wadsworth endowed his native Hartford, Davis was obviously in need of no one to correct his instincts.

One of his earliest Gothic essays, long since demolished, was Glen Ellen, the seat at Towson, Maryland, of Robert Gilmor, grandson of an East India trader. While touring the Old World, young Gilmor had called on Scott at Abbotsford, bringing back a cane presented to him by Scott himself, and so was perfectly prepared for the medieval romance that Davis drafted. But Davis was equally successful with H. K. Harral, a leather merchant from Charleston, South Carolina, who moved his business to Bridgeport, Connecticut. Harral's Walnut Wood, completed in 1846, was an ideal advertisement of the Gothic: its plan was informal, and not even Downing could have complained that the apparent stone facade was actually bricks plastered over. Generously willed to the people of Bridgeport by Archer C. Wheeler, its last owner, Walnut Wood could have become an ideal pilgrimage center if a stubborn mayor, with ideas of his own, had not decided to pull it down to make way for a parking lot.

But the most expensive of all Davis's houses is still with us: Lyndhurst, the marble palace he began building in 1838 for William Paulding, brother of Martin Van Buren's Secretary of the Navy, at Tarrytown on the Hudson. It was later acquired by Jay Gould, who had come to love the Gothic while selecting the cottages adorning the corners of the map of Albany County which he peddled long before he raped the Erie. Gould's daughter, the Duchess of Talleyrand, made the estate over to the National Trust, and now anyone may

18
Above is the original sketch for
Glen Ellen (1832), residence of
Robert Gilmore, Towson,
Maryland.
At right are a sketch and a floor
plan of Glen Ellen as it was
actually built; the third story was
never erected. The building was
eventually demolished. Photo:
Metropolitan Museum of Art.

DWELLING, EXECUTED FOR ROBT. GILMOR ESQ. NEAR BALTIMORE.

Town & Davis, 1832. Lower design as executed for Robt. Gilmor, jr near Baltimore

catch a glance of the superb dining room where Gould gazed at his favorite orchids before pondering what could be accomplished with the treasury of the next railroad at his command.

New York's Mayor Philip Hone, who made a point of calling at every house of consequence in and out of the city, was distressed by what he took to be Paulding's extravagance. A wiser critic might have observed that Davis could turn an oriel window as subtly as Pugin at Scarisbrick, but to Hone, Lyndhurst resembled "a Gothic monastery, with towers, turrets and trellises, minarets, mosaics and mouseholes, archways, armories and airholes, peaked windows and pinnacled roofs, and many other fantasies too tedious to enumerate, the whole constituting an edifice of gigantic size, with no room in it, great cost and little comfort, which, if I mistake not, will one of these days be designated as *Paulding's Folly.*"

Downing knew better. "I have never seen anything to equal it," he told Davis. "I think together we can build up a large business," he was writing a little later, aware that his friend had already created another castle, plaster-coated this time, for General Philip Saint George Cocke in Powhatan County, Virginia. General Cocke also had the courtesy to have Davis design the barracks, the mess hall and the officers' quarters at Virginia Military Institute. The barracks were burned in the war, but Stonewall Jackson had trained his cadets on the lawn, and the barracks were rightly rebuilt when the war was over. By then General Cocke was no more, having committed suicide on Christmas Day, 1861. His estate, Belmead, later a Roman Catholic school for boys, is currently slated for demolition.

There are—or rather, there were—dozens of other choice examples of Davis Gothic. One of these that has so far escaped the bulldozers is the house in New Bedford, Massachusetts, of the mill owner William J. Rotch. Its symmetry may disappoint those who prefer the more intricate massing of Lyndhurst or Belmead, but its brick façade meant much to the architect, who took the trouble to defend its hipped roof in a letter to *The Horticulturalist.* Such a roof, he wrote, "is precisely what I have been taught to consider as desirable in a rural *cottage* residence, though rarely found in country houses. May I say that they do not sufficiently *spread themselves?*" He was arguing in favor of the low-slung horizontal lines that Wright would emphasize in his prairie houses—and arguing with the blessing of John Ruskin, whose chapter on Truth in *The Seven Lamps of Architecture* he quoted in justification.

With the coming of the Civil War, Davis was to feel out of date. "Examined some of the latest buildings on Broadway," he commented in his diary for July 1, 1861, "most of which are depraved in the extreme, corrupt in all their parts." He was, he confessed, particularly depressed by the Gothic arches he spotted over the Ionic columns of Brooks Brothers' store on the corner of Grand Street. He spoke as the acknowledged master of his generation, no matter if he designed next to no churches.

19
Gate Lodge at Llewellyn Park
(1857), West Orange, New
Jersey. Architect, Alexander
Jackson Davis. Davis's own
house within the grounds has
been demolished. Photo:
Wayne Andrews.

20
Lyndhurst (1838 – 65),
residence of William Paulding,
Tarrytown, New York. Architect,
Alexander Jackson Davis. Later
enlarged for George Merritt, the
estate was acquired in 1880 by
Jay Gould, the one-time master
of the Erie Railroad. Open to the
public by the National Trust for
Historic Preservation. Photo:
Wayne Andrews.

21
New York University (1833 –
35), New York City; demolished.
Arthitects, Town & Davis. As
painted in an Allegorical
Landscape, by S. F. B. Morse.
Photo: New-York Historical
Society.

22
Entrance to Wadsworth
Atheneum (1842), Hartford,
Connecticut. Architects, Town &
Davis. Photo: Wayne Andrews.

23
Walnut Wood (1846), residence
of H. K. Harral, Bridgeport,
Connecticut; demolished.
Architect, Alexander Jackson
Davis. For Harral, Davis
designed even a Gothic tomb in
the local cemetery. Photo:
Wayne Andrews.

24
Parlor at Walnut Wood (1846),
residence of H. K. Harral,
Bridgeport, Connecticut.
Architect, Alexander Jackson
Davis. The statue of Pandora is
the work of Chauncey Ives.
Photo: Wayne Andrews.

25
Gothic bedroom at Walnut
Wood (1846), residence of H. K.
Harral, Bridgeport,
Connecticut. Architect,
Alexander Jackson Davis.
Photo: Wayne Andrews.

26
Dining room at Lyndhurst
(1838 – 65), residence of
William Paulding, Tarrytown,
New York. Architect, Alexander
Jackson Davis. Photo:
Wayne Andrews.
27
Belmead (1845), residence of
General Philip Saint George
Cocke, Powhatan County,
Virginia. Architect, Alexander
Jackson Davis. Photo:
Wayne Andrews.

28
Barracks (1851), Virginia
Military Institute, Lexington,
Virginia. Architect, Alexander
Jackson Davis. Also surviving is
the Commandant's House by
Davis. Photo: Wayne Andrews.

29
Elwanger & Barry Nurseries
Office (1854), Rochester, New
York. Architect, Alexander
Jackson Davis. Photo:
Wayne Andrews.

30
Residence (1850) of William J.
Rotch, New Bedford,
Massachusetts. Architect,
Alexander Jackson Davis.
Photo: Wayne Andrews.

*Original clubhouse (1846) of
the New York Yacht Club,
Hoboken, New Jersey. Architect,
Alexander Jackson Davis. When
this photograph was taken, the
clubhouse had been removed to
Glen Cove, Long Island. Today
it stands in Mystic, Connecticut.
Photo: Wayne Andrews.*

32
Residence (1845) of the attorney
C. B. Sedgwick, Syracuse, New
York; demolished. Architect,
Alexander Jackson Davis.
Photo: Wayne Andrews.

The prominent ecclesiastical architect of the time was Richard Upjohn, a high-minded native of Dorsetshire who, at the age of twenty-seven, came to America in 1829, having served his apprenticeship to a cabinetmaker. Although his wife was the daughter of a dissenting minister, he was himself a High Church Anglican—and almost as devout as Pugin, which was a blessing for the Episcopal Church he served so splendidly. "The object is not to surprise with novelties in church architecture," he reasoned, "but to make what is to be made truly ecclesiastical—a temple of solemnities—such as will fix the attention of persons, and make them respond in heart and spirit to the opening service—*The Lord is in his holy temple, let all the earth keep silence.*"

He fought for deep chancels with the fire that Pugin spent on rood screens, and it was really not at all surprising that he declined the opportunity to design a Unitarian church for the Bostonians. "Can we point out anywhere a class of men whose private life is more pure?" urged Theodore Lyman, an Anglican for whom he contrived a house in Brookline. But Lyman wrote in vain. Later on, when Upjohn did manage to create a church in Brooklyn for the Presbyterians, one of his fellow architects understood that he had done it conscientiously, "upon the ground that Presbyterians were not entitled to architecture."

He was to know hard times before becoming the preeminent architect of the Episcopal Church. "All my business is gone—all my means—and nearly all my credit," he was writing Richard Hallowell Gardiner in the fall of 1837. Could Gardiner—married after all to the sister of Frederic Tudor, the man who cornered the market for ice in Boston—possibly forward fifty bushels of potatoes or three or four barrels of apples? For Gardiner in 1835 he designed Oaklands, a stone Gothic villa in Gardiner, Maine, that Nathaniel Hawthorne thought "well deserves the name of castle or palace." Oaklands must not be slighted, but it may not have been so brilliant an example of the Gothic as the frame cottage he fashioned in Newport for Gardiner's brother-in-law George Noble Jones, a Georgia planter who favored the Rhode Island climate in summer.

Who knows, Upjohn might have challenged Davis himself as a domestic architect. But to Upjohn, churches came first. "People may be as fantastic as they please in their dwellings," he conceded, "but in the Church of God, they have no right to show off their follies, notwithstanding they may be owners of pews." He approved of good crimson damask for seats and cushions, which he fancied would form the proper contrast to the black walnut pews.

It is obvious that he approached any ecclesiastical commission in a mood of humility—only this could account for the care he lavished on dozens of frame churches for country towns—but no matter how humble he might be, he never neglected the commands of piety. When he went to work on Trinity, New York, the biggest job of his career, he first made sure that the chancel would be deep, and then, without consulting anyone, climbed to the top of the spire

33
Oaklands (1835 – 36), residence
of Richard Hallowell Gardiner,
Gardiner, Maine. Architect,
Richard Upjohn. Photo:
Wayne Andrews.

34
Residence (1838) of George
Noble Jones, Newport, Rhode
Island. Architect, Richard
Upjohn. Open to the public by
the Preservation Society of
Newport. Photo:
Wayne Andrews.

35
Trinity Church (1839 – 46),
New York City. Architect,
Richard Upjohn. Photo:
Wayne Andrews.
36
Church of the Holy Communion
(1844 – 45), New York City.
Architect, Richard Upjohn.
Photo: Wayne Andrews.

37
Church of the Ascension
(1840 – 41), New York City.
Architect, Richard Upjohn.
Photo: Wayne Andrews.
38
St. Mary's Church (1846 – 54),
Burlington, New Jersey.
Architect, Richard Upjohn.
Photo: Wayne Andrews.

39
Interior, St. Mary's Church
(1846 – 54), Burlington, New
Jersey. Architect, Richard
Upjohn. Photo:
Wayne Andrews.

and set a cross in place, taking care to pull down the scaffolding before the Low Church element could tell what had gone on.

Trinity, dedicated in the spring of 1846, made the perfect impression on Downing. Writing in *The Horticulturalist*, he advised his audience that it would "stand as far above all other Gothic structures of the kind in this country, as a Raphael's madonna before a tolerable sign painting." Downing, who may have known that Upjohn made sketches for a trussed roof, found no fault with Trinity's plaster vaulting, and perhaps the only artist to be disappointed was Thomas Cole. He yearned to paint its altarpiece. "But I suppose I am talking of what must not be; we are too much fettered by puritanical opinion to allow us to place an altarpiece, even in Trinity Church," he complained to Gulian Verplanck.

It seems more than likely that Upjohn glanced at a Pugin sketch for an ideal church before completing this dressed stone masterpiece, although it must be remembered that the sketch in question was not published until 1841, two years after this essay in the Perpendicular or late Gothic was begun. He switched to the Decorated or earlier Gothic for the Church of the Holy Communion on Sixth Avenue and Twenty-sixth Street, erected in 1845, and Decorated, too, was the Church of the Ascension on Fifth Avenue. Here he had his troubles with the Low Church rector Manton Eastburn, who, behind his back, bought up all the land to the rear in order to frustrate anything so papistical as a deep chancel.

Upjohn was to have a freer hand at St. Mary's in Burlington, New Jersey, where Bishop George Washington Doane, remembered for the words to the hymn "Fling Out the Banner," was so bold as to disregard the advice of the Cambridge Camden Society over in England. They insisted he should build a replica of St. John's, Shottesbrook, while he considered that something of Upjohn's own invention in the Early English style was preferable.

Upjohn's chief rival in the ecclesiastical domain, James Renwick, Jr., was not half so serious, but may be said to have earned the two steam yachts, one for offshore cruises and the other for important destinations, on which he rested from his labors. "Nature cut him out for a boss carpenter," fumed the diarist George Templeton Strong, who ranted all too often against his "pasteboard imitations," never realizing that Renwick, whose mother was a Brevoort and whose wife was an Aspinwall, had more than social connections to recommend him.

At twenty-five, in 1843, Renwick won the competition for Grace Church on Broadway, a subtle creation in marble for the Episcopalians that owed not a little to his study of Pugin. "This is to be the fashionable church," Mayor Hone recorded on its consecration in 1846. "Already its aisles are filled (especially on Sundays after morning services in other churches) with gay parties of ladies in feathers and mousseline-de-laine dresses, and dandies with moustaches and high-heeled boots; the lofty arches resound with astute criticisms upon Gothic architecture from fair ladies who have had the advantage of foreign travel, and scientific remarks upon acoustics from elderly millionaires who do not hear quite so well as formerly."

Renwick was not quite so subtle in St. Patrick's Cathedral for the Romans, on which he worked from 1858 to 1879. A more extravagant example of his imagination was the Gothic castle in Syracuse which he finished in 1851 for a certain C. T. Longstreet, the first to think of shipping ready-made suits to California during the Gold Rush. The castle's mirrored staircase, which might not have offended William Beckford, was ultimately appreciated by the students of Syracuse University's School of Journalism, but the university, which could not be bothered with the preservation of a national monument, destroyed it the moment the campus became crowded after the Second World War.

One more distinguished Gothic church of the era should be mentioned: Holy Trinity on Brooklyn Heights, New York, the work of Minard Lafever, a one-time carpenter from Morristown, New Jersey, who published a number of invaluable builders' guides that acquainted craftsmen with the most delicate details, both Grecian and Gothic. Only the Gothic fascinated the Anglican paper manufacturer Edgar John Bartow, who raised the funds for his Decorated monument in Haverstraw red sandstone which was opened in 1847.

If churches could be Gothic, so could prisons, and the English-born John Haviland, who began his career in Russia, where he made a friend of our minister John Quincy Adams, devoted most of his life to American jails of medieval appearance. His most famous was Eastern State Penitentiary in Philadelphia. This was ready for business in the summer of 1829, and was instantly noted by penologists for being the first in the world to display corridors leading from a central observation point. It was also the first to carry out the principles upheld by the leaders of the Philadelphia Society for Alleviating the Miseries of Prisons, who had come to the conclusion that solitary confinement was the best possible fate for a convict. Separation, they argued, could not fail to stimulate a prisoner's conscience.

Charles Dickens, who visited Eastern in 1842, was far from impressed by the blessings of solitary confinement. He paid next to no attention to Haviland's gateway, with its massive wrought-iron portcullis and double oaken doors studded with iron rivets. Instead, he reported the fits of trembling that seized prisoners so fortunate as to be released. It was like a complete derangement of the nervous system, one of the guards told him. And Dickens could not forget that "over the head and face of every prisoner who comes into this melancholy house, a black hood is drawn; and in this dark shroud, an emblem of the curtain dropped between him and the living world, he is led to the cell from which he never again comes forth, until the whole term of imprisonment has expired."

*40
Residence (1851) of C. T.
Longstreet, Syracuse, New York;
demolished. Architect, James
Renwick, Jr. Photo: Wayne
Andrews.*

41
*Residence (1859) of David Dale
Owen, New Harmony, Indiana.
Architects, James Renwick, Jr.,
and David Dale Owen. The
geologist David Dale Owen was
the brother of Robert Dale Owen
of the socialist colony who
defended Renwick's
Romanesque design for the
Smithsonian in his Hints on
Public Architecture. Photo:
Wayne Andrews.*
42
*Rectory (1847), Grace Church,
New York City. Architect, James
Renwick, Jr. Photo:
Wayne Andrews.*

43
Grace Church (1843 – 46), New York City. Architect, James Renwick, Jr. Photo: Wayne Andrews.
44
St. Patrick's Cathedral (1858 – 76), New York City. Architect, James Renwick, Jr. Photo: Rockefeller Center Inc.

45
*Eastern State Penitentiary
(1829), Philadelphia,
Pennsylvania. Architect, John
Haviland. Photo:
Wayne Andrews.*
46
*Holy Trinity Church (1847),
Brooklyn, New York. Architect,
Minard Lafever. Photo:
Wayne Andrews.*

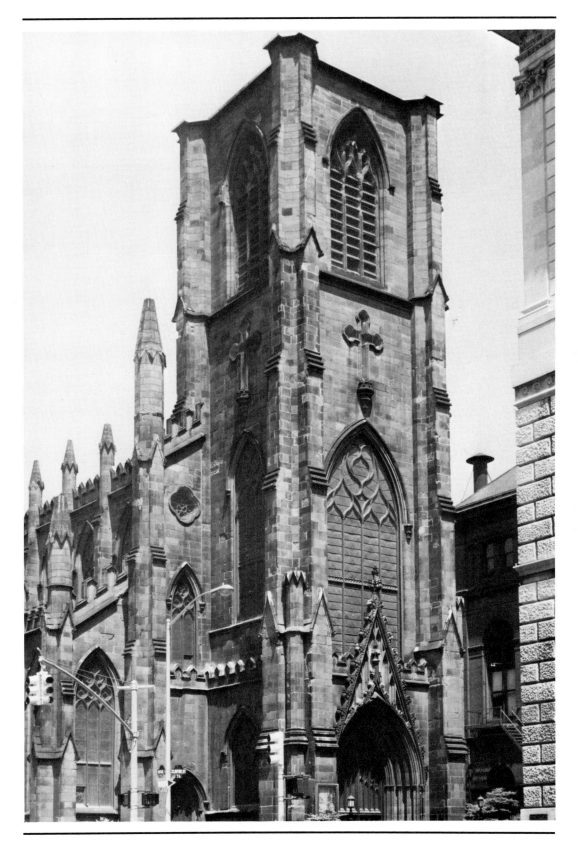

47
*Interior, Holy Trinity Church
(1847), Brooklyn, New York.
Architect, Minard Lafever.
Photo: Wayne Andrews.*
48
*Lancaster County Jail (1850),
Lancaster, Pennsylvania.
Architect, John Haviland.
Photo: Wayne Andrews.*

Our prisons were only one indication of the extent of the victory won by Downing. The Gothic was irresistible in the years from Jackson to Lincoln, and California was no sooner acquired than General Mariano Vallejo, one of the Spaniards easily reconciled to American rule, built himself a delightful Gothic cottage with tea house at Sonoma that Downing *should* have illustrated in one of his books. Vallejo's Lachrima Montis was actually "built" in New England and shipped to the coast in the first possible steamer.

New England itself surrendered, as could be proved by the Wedding Cake House in Kennebunk, Maine, where a clever carpenter in the early fifties hung Gothic tracery over an innocent brick house dating from the beginning of the century. In fact, the fashion was so firmly fixed in New England that even after the Civil War, when the summer colony at Oak Bluffs on Martha's Vineyard was planned, nothing but the Gothic would do for those rows of cottages.

And in the South, General Cocke was not the only solid citizen to prefer a medieval mansion. Charles Bruce of Virginia, son of the James Bruce who apparently made a million and a half out of country stores and tobacco before he died in 1837, was no sooner graduated from Harvard and returned from a grand tour of Europe than he had a certain John Johnson build him Staunton Hill, a plastered fortress that today belongs to his grandson David K. E. Bruce, our first ambassador to Communist China. It is perhaps only just to add that the Bruces were not exclusively Gothic in their taste. Not far away in Halifax County, Charles's cousin James Coles Bruce decided on a Doric temple for his Berry Hill in 1848.

The Bruces had their landholdings in Louisiana, and must have traveled in that direction, which may be one reason why the Gothic spread so easily to the Deep South. James Harrison Dakin, a graduate of the Davis office, has been suggested as having been the designer of Afton Villa, the plantation house of David Barrow at St. Francisville. In any event he was to make the most of his opportunities when he planned the capitol at Baton Rouge in 1847. Unaware at the time he was experiencing life on the Mississippi that he would one day come down with the Gothic contagion himself, Mark Twain was perplexed by Dakin's daring. "Sir Walter Scott is probably responsible for the capitol building," he claimed, "for it is not conceivable that this little sham castle would ever have been built, if he had not run the people mad, a couple of generations ago, with his mediaeval romances. The South has not yet recovered from the debilitating influence of his books . . .

"By itself," Mark Twain went on, "the imitation castle is doubtless harmless, and well enough; but as a symbol and breeder and sustainer of maudlin Middle-Age romanticism here in the midst of the plainest and sturdiest and infinitely greatest and worthiest of all centuries the world has seen, it is necessarily a hurtful thing and a mistake."

Perhaps. But to Americans of our time, who have to face in almost every city the impersonal curtain-wall skyscrapers of Skidmore, Owings & Merrill and their imitators, the individualism of the Gothic in the age of Downing is a welcome sight. They were no archaeologists, the revivalists of those days. They may have looked foolish to Mark Twain, but at least they spoke for themselves as no computer could.

It is a shame that Davis failed to add the Adams family to the list of his clients. He tried hard to convince Charles Francis Adams, but the only result of the call he paid at Quincy in the fall of 1845 was a sick headache he got from the cordial offered by old John Quincy Adams. That, and the chance to observe Henry and Brooks Adams long before they reached Harvard. "Children very disorderly and noisy," runs the entry in his diary.

49
*Gazebo (1858), Temelec Hall,
residence of Granville Swift,
Sonoma, California. Architect
unknown. Swift, who made his
money in the Gold Rush, was
also prominent in the Bear Flag
Revolt of 1846, which somewhat
prematurely proclaimed
California's independence from
Mexico. Photo: Wayne Andrews.*
50
*The Lace House (c. 1860),
Blackhawk, Colorado. Architect
unknown. Photo:
Wayne Andrews.*

51
Residence (1881) of E. J.
"Lucky" Baldwin, Arcadia,
California. Architect, A. A.
Bennett. Although erected long
after the age of Downing, this
villa for one of the plungers of
the Comstock Lode betrays
Downing's influence — and also
that of Charles Locke Eastlake,
the English historian of the
Gothic revival who had ideas of
his own on the subject of
decoration. Open to the public.
Photo: Wayne Andrews.

52
Residence (c. 1851) of John M.
Wheeler, Ann Arbor, Michigan;
sadly altered since this
photograph was taken. Architect
unknown. Photo:
Wayne Andrews.

53
House of the Seven Gables
(1850?), Busti, New York.
Architect unknown. Photo:
Wayne Andrews.

54
Gate Lodge (c. 1840),
Netherwood, residence of James
Lenox, New Hamburg, New
York. Architect unknown. Hone,
who came to call in 1850, by
which time Netherwood belonged
to Gardiner G. Howland of the
shipping dynasty, was pleased to
record that the Howlands,
"hitherto so tenacious of strict
religious observances, consented
to receive the singer Jenny Lind
on a Sunday. Netherwood,
pronounced by Hone to be "a
princely residence," has been
demolished. Photo:
Wayne Andrews.

55
Fonthill (1848), residence of
Edwin Forrest, New York City.
Architect unknown. Now the
library of the College of Saint
Mary in the Bronx, this castle
calling Beckford to the attention
of the New World was built by
the great ham actor of the day, a
man who spent $200,000
divorcing his wife in his
inimitable manner. Forrest had
no use for the English actor
William Charles Macready.
When Macready invaded the
New York stage, Forrest
provoked the Astor Place Opera
House riot, in which several
hundred were injured and
twenty-two killed. The divorce
cost so much that Forrest was
obliged to sell his castle. Photo:
Wayne Andrews.

56
Neff Cottage (c. 1845),
Gambier, Ohio. Architect
unknown. Photo:
Wayne Andrews.

57
Ingleside (1852), residence of
Henry Boone Ingles, Lexington,
Kentucky. Architect, John
McMurtry. Ingles was the son-
in-law of a prosperous iron-
foundry man. His architect had
supervised the construction of
Loudoun, a Gothic villa by
Alexander Jackson Davis, also
in Lexington. Photo:
Wayne Andrews.

58
Church of the Cross (c. 1850),
Bluffton, South Carolina.
Architect, E. B. White. Photo:
Wayne Andrews.

59
*Residence (c. 1845) of H. C.
Bowen, Woodstock, Connecticut.
Architect, Joseph C. Wells. Open
to the public by the Society for the
Preservation of New England
Antiquities. Bowen was the
publisher of Henry Ward
Beecher's journal, The
Independent. The English-
born Wells was also the architect
of the Gothic First Presbyterian
Church of Fifth Avenue, New
York. Photo: Wayne Andrews.*

60
Brokenstraw (c. 1840),
residence of William Irvine,
Irvine, Pennsylvania;
demolished. Architect unknown.
Photo: Wayne Andrews.

61
*Residence (1847) of Henry Ten
Eyck, Cazenovia, New York.
Architect unknown. This
reverent example of Downing's
influence serves as Cazenovia's
Town Hall. Photo:
Wayne Andrews.*
62
*Residence (c. 1848) of J. B.
Chollar, Watervliet, New York;
demolished. Architect unknown.
This house was a favorite with
Jay Gould when he was
beginning his business career.
He illustrated it on his map of
Albany County. Photo:
Wayne Andrews.*

63
Residence (1858) of Dr. Charles
Bonner, Holly Springs,
Mississippi. Architect unknown.
Photo: Wayne Andrews.

64
Gothic cottage (c. 1868), Oak
Bluffs, Martha's Vineyard,
Massachusetts. Architect
unknown. One of the dozen or
more surviving of the Methodist
summer colony. Photo:
Wayne Andrews.

65
The Wedding Cake House (c.
1850), Kennebunk, Maine.
Architect unknown. Photo:
Wayne Andrews.

66
Residence (c. 1840) of John Schoolcraft, Jr., Guilderland, New York. Architect unknown. This Schoolcraft was the uncle of the explorer Henry Rowe Schoolcraft. Photo: Wayne Andrews.

67
*Green-Meldrim House (1856),
Savannah, Georgia. Architect
unknown. Here lived Charles
Green, the English-born
grandfather of the novelist
Julien Green. "I was humiliated
by this simple dwelling," reported
Julien Green, who came to
Savannah after living all his life
in Paris. "But when I drew near,
I changed my mind. It is well
proportioned and not without a
certain grandeur." Photo:
Wayne Andrews.*

68
Staunton Hill (1848), residence
of Charles Bruce, Charlotte
County, Virginia. Architect,
John Johnson. Photo:
Wayne Andrews.

69
Athenwood (1850), residence of
Thomas Waterman Wood, which
he designed, in Montpelier,
Vermont. Wood was an artist
whose paintings are piously
preserved in a museum named
after him in Montpelier. Photo:
Wayne Andrews.

70
Glimmerstone (1849),
Cavendish, Vermont. Architect,
Lucius Page. Photo:
Wayne Andrews.

71
Afton Villa (1849), residence of
David Barrow, St. Francisville,
Louisiana. Architect, James
Harrison Dakin (?). Dakin may
have been in charge of the
Gothic remodeling of this
plantation house, destroyed by
fire in 1963. Photo:
Wayne Andrews.

72
The Capitol (1847 – 50), Baton Rouge, Louisiana. Architect, James Harrison Dakin. The cast-iron vaulting in the interior was added in 1880 by William Freret, the architect in charge of restoration. Photo: Wayne Andrews.

Gothic
Afternoon

"At this day," wrote John Ruskin in 1885 on beginning his autobiography, "though I have kind invitations enough to visit America, I could not, even for a couple of months, live in a country so miserable as to possess no castles." That there were castles in America, that Davis, Renwick and the others had done their best, was a fact that Ruskin dismissed. Like a journalist turning out copy under pressure, he could erase from his mind any fact that did not apply to his present assignment. Not that he was a journalist. He wrote the most passionate prose in English on the subject of architecture, and there is no doubt he deserved both his fame and his audience, even though his constant aim, like that of so many museum curators and professors, was to escape from life into art.

Henry James understood this. "In face, in manner, in talk, in mind, he is weakness pure and simple," James reported in 1869. "I use the word, not invidiously but scientifically. He has the beauties of his defects; but to see him only confirms the impression given by his writing, that he has been scared back by the grim face of reality into the world of unreason and illusion, and that he wanders there without a compass or guide, or any light save the fitful flashes of his beautiful genius."

The childhood of this Goth would terrify a seasoned psychiatrist. "The horror of Sunday," he recollected, "used even to cast its prescient gloom as far back into the week as Friday—and all the glory of Monday, with church seven days removed again, was not equivalent for it." His mother, beginning every day by reading the Bible with him, did not approve of toys, although he was allowed a bunch of jingling keys, a cart, a ball, and two boxes of wooden bricks. He was whipped frequently, often for making the mistake of falling downstairs. His father, who rarely entertained, fearing that he might come in contact with his social superiors, took particular care not to hire clever clerks to assist him in the family sherry business: they might challenge his supremacy.

"I was not the sort of creature," Ruskin confessed, "that a boy would care much for, or indeed any human being, except Papa and Mama." When he went up to Oxford, his mother came along to watch over him. She had thought he might become a bishop, and must have warned him of what to expect in Paris when he went there. It was not until the winter of 1844, when he was twenty-five, that he was able to look at the religious pictures in the Louvre without the proper Protestant revulsion, and when he was a grown man, he made a point of covering all the pictures he owned with special screens on Sundays. The holiness of the Sabbath was to be preserved at all cost.

"I believe I once had affections as warm as most people," he said. "But partly from evil chance, and partly from foolish misplacing of them, they have got tumbled down and broken into pieces. It is a very great, in the long run the greatest, misfortune of my life that, on the whole, my relations, cousins and so forth, are persons with whom I can have no sympathy, and that circumstances have always somehow or another kept me out of the way of people of whom I could have made friends. So that I have no friendships and no loves . . . There is an old glove in one of my drawers that has lain there eighteen years, which is worth something to me yet."

In spite of this he was married in 1848 to Effie Gray, a luckless girl from Edinburgh, born in the very room where Ruskin's own grandfather committed suicide. "I think you would soon find great delight in deciphering inscriptions—interpreting devices—and unravelling enigmas," he wrote her during their engagement. "Gradually I think you might become far, far my superior in judging of dates and styles." Once they were married, he made a habit of pinning lists of her faults on her pincushion, but the marriage was never consummated, and in 1854 it was annulled. "Perhaps for *my health*," he revealed, "it might be better that I should declare at once I wanted to be a Protestant monk, separate from my wife."

Father and Mother Ruskin easily persuaded themselves that Effie was suffering from a nervous ailment. She wasn't. She was eventually married to the painter Sir John Everett Millais, with whom she was able to lead a normal life. The disaster of the marriage that was not a marriage might have kept another man from seeking the company of women, but Ruskin was an incorrigible angelist. He was later to fall in love, in his fashion, with Rose La Touche, only nine when she was first brought to call at Denmark Hill, the Ruskin mansion. But her mother, who must have heard why Effie Gray had to leave her husband, could not bear the thought of Rose's suffering Effie's fate and burned every letter she could from Ruskin to her daughter. He proposed to her when she was seventeen and he forty-seven, but she died unmarried and insane. Ruskin was to lose his own mind: he died in the belief that Rose had become his bride.

The only friend of Ruskin—the only man with whom he could talk about what was troubling him—was Charles Eliot Norton, the American who believed that all art had come to an end in 1600, but was nevertheless the first to teach the history of art at Harvard College. Norton did not presume to investigate Ruskin's passionate lack of passion for Rose La Touche. "She loved him, but refused to be his wife," he decided, "because, holding a strict evangelical creed, she could not make up her mind to marry a skeptic."

The faithful Norton was just the man in just the position to spread Ruskin's gospel in the New World. Although he never hesitated to speak out on almost any subject—he reminded Edith Wharton that "no great work of the imagination has ever been based on illicit passion" and even as late as 1901 was positive that Theodore Roosevelt did not possess "the art and craft by which popularity is to be gained"—he never could talk back to Ruskin. "He has always been perverse and irrational," he admitted in 1883, "and he does not grow less so, but his heart has all its old sweetness." There were rewards for

Norton's subservience. When he came to Denmark Hill, Father Ruskin offered him a glass of the very sherry Lord Nelson kept aboard the *Victory*, and was even allowed to observe Mother Ruskin's "quaint, decided moral way . . ." Her son, he recalled, "ventured occasionally to be playful with her with a lively humor which occasionally ruffled her, but which, on the whole, she did not dislike."

For a critic, Ruskin traveled with a lot of baggage. Although he idolized the work of Turner, he never glanced at the French Impressionists who carried on where Turner left off, and when he came upon Whistler's quite Turner-esque view of the fireworks in Cremorne Gardens, offered an insult so foul that Whistler had to sue him. And at almost any moment he might fly into a diatribe against the Roman Catholic Church. He even held the Romans responsible for the gloom he discovered on mountaintops. "The atheism or dissipation of a large portion of the population in crowded capitals prevents this gloom from being felt in full force; but it resumes its power in mountain solitudes over the minds of the comparatively ignorant and more suffering peasantry." No wonder he believed that Pugin did not deserve to be considered an architect. "Employ him by all means, but on small work," he recommended. "Expect no cathedrals from him; but no one, at present can design a better finial."

What may have particularly endeared Ruskin to Norton was that he never could tell where art began or morals ended. "This is the great enigma of art history," he assumed, "that you must not follow art without pleasure, nor must you follow it for the sake of pleasure." It was evident that he was not looking simply for a good time when he announced the two virtues of building—first, the sign of man's good work; and secondly, the expression of man's delight in his work.

In his loathing of the Renaissance he left Pugin far behind. "No building," he said, "could be really admirable which was not admirable to the poor." And what was the Renaissance but a snob's paradise? "The Gothic," he maintained, "had fellowship with all hearts, and was universal, like nature: it could frame a temple for the prayer of nations, or shrink into the poor man's winding stair. But here"—he was referring to the misdeeds of Alberti and his successors—"was an architecture that would not shrink, that had in it no submission, no mercy. The proud princes and the lords rejoiced in it. It was full of insult to the poor in every line."

Ruskin could be silly. He could also transmit his convictions. "It is impossible," he proclaimed in 1849 in his *Seven Lamps of Architecture*, "to restore anything that has ever been great and beautiful in architecture . . . Restoration . . . means the total destruction of what a building can suffer." He went on to plead that "the greatest glory of a building is not in its stones, or in its gold. Its greatest glory is in its age, and in that deep sense of voicefulness, of stern watching, of mysterious sympathy, nay, even of approval or condemnation, which we feel in walls that have been long washed by the passing waves of humanity . . . It is in that golden stain of time, that we are to look for the real light, and color and preciousness of architecture."

As a poet, he understood that "no architecture can be truly noble which is not imperfect." The Gothic was eternally attractive because of man's love of change. "It is," he explained in 1851 in *The Stones of Venice*, "that strange disquietude of the Gothic spirit that is its greatness; that restlessness of the dreaming mind, that wanders hither and thither among the niches and flickers feverishly around the pinnacles and frets and fades in labyrinthine knots and shadows along wall and roof, and yet is not satisfied, nor shall be satisfied. The Greek could stay in his triglyph furrow, and be at peace, but the work of the Gothic heart is fretwork still, and it can neither rest in, nor from its labor, but must pass on sleeplessly, until its love of change shall be pacified forever in the change that must come alike on them that wake and them that sleep."

Ruskin believed that the only style proper for modern work was the Northern Gothic of the thirteenth century as seen in England and France, and in 1849 was saying that the Venetian Gothic was not the most noble but only one among many early schools. But he was to be forever identified with the Venetian Gothic. "It is in Venice, and in Venice only," he declared in 1851, "that effectual blows can be struck at this pestilent art of the Renaissance. Destroy its claims to admiration there, and it can assert them nowhere else."

The most striking example of Ruskin's influence in England was the University Museum at Oxford, begun in 1855 to designs furnished by the firm of Deane and Woodward. Ruskin acted as adviser and had no real reason to complain. In fact he was mortified. "There is a discouraging aspect of parsimony about it," he grumbled. He also complained about all the other English specimens of Venetian Gothic. By the third edition of the *Stones of Venice* he could detect the power of his prose "on nearly every cheap villa-builder between Denmark Hill and Bromley." One reason he gave for moving out of his house was that "it was surrounded by the accursed Frankenstein monsters of, indirectly, [my] own making."

The 1860s were hardly upon us when his word was taken as gospel by the architects of the United States. What is curious, and might have puzzled Ruskin himself, is the relationship between many of his American followers and the foundation of what we call modern architecture. Ruskinian monuments may look like yesterday, but many of their creators looked toward tomorrow.

We might as well confess that the Venetian Gothic capitol of Connecticut, hailed in 1885 by the readers of the *American Architect and Building News* as one of the ten best buildings of the United States, does not seem to lead us down the path we have just pointed out. This was the work of Richard Upjohn's son Richard Michell Upjohn, who has yet to be associated with what is known as the modern movement. Nor does Stuart Hall of the seminary at Princeton, dating from 1876, buttress our argument. This was designed by

73
The University Museum
(1855 – 60), Oxford. Architects,
Deane & Woodward. Photo:
Wayne Andrews.

William Alexander Potter, whose only claim to being "advanced" is that he later followed in the wake of H. H. Richardson, the best of his achievements in the Richardsonian manner being St. Mary's Church at Tuxedo Park, New York. Nor does Mark Twain's house at Hartford, planned by William Alexander's brother Edward Tuckerman Potter, qualify, aside from its interiors by Louis C. Tiffany, as the landmark of a modern man, although the powerful polychromy of its brick facade testifies to the attention paid by the architect to Ruskin's praise of color bands for aging a new building.

But when we come to Frank Furness, the uncompromising Philadelphian famous for so many alarming banks, we are in the presence of a man who exercised a real fascination on Louis Sullivan. Furness and his partner, Hewitt, were at work on the emphatically Venetian Gothic Pennsylvania Academy of the Fine Arts when Sullivan, just out of MIT, stopped by to ask for a job. "Louis was a fool," said Furness, "to have wasted his time in a place where one was filled with sawdust, like a doll, and became a prig, a snob and an ass." Which was just the sort of reprimand that Sullivan enjoyed to the full. He was to wander off to Chicago and his future when the Depression of 1873 forced Furness & Hewitt to fire him, but he would never forget the short time he spent in that office. "Standards were so high," he remembered, "talent was so manifestly taken for granted, and the atmosphere the free and easy one of a true workshop savoring of the guild where craftsmanship was paramount and personal."

Another American who caught Ruskin's message was Peter Bonnett Wight, who in 1863 recollected the doges' palace in designing New York's National Academy of Design. This has vanished, as has the equally Ruskinian library that he completed on Brooklyn Heights, but Wight will not be easily forgotten. Moving to Chicago in 1872, he was to train two giants in the art of designing skyscrapers, Daniel Hudson Burnham and John Wellborn Root. Wight's one-time partner, Russell Sturgis, must also be remembered, and for more than his Gothic work on the Yale campus. He turned critic in his later years; well aware that the firm of McKim, Mead & White had fallen into mortal sin by abandoning its early, original style in favor of a revival of the Italian Renaissance, he denounced its Renaissance recollections in terms that even Ruskin could not have bettered. Reviewing its palaces in 1895, he declared that "in general, the buildings which we have been considering, taken together, are as good as can be expected of any firm which is doing all the work it can get."

Still another American who adored Ruskin was James Lyman Silsbee, who surprised Syracuse, New York, in 1876 with a Venetian Gothic savings bank, still standing and still honored. Like Wight, he enjoyed a second career in Chicago, where he had the prescience to offer Frank Lloyd Wright his first job. Wright, normally not the most charitable man where other architects were concerned, never forgot the opportunity that Silsbee gave him. "He had

74
The Capitol (1878), Hartford,
Connecticut. Architect, Richard
Michell Upjohn. Photo: Wayne
Andrews.

75
Residence (1874) of Samuel
Clemens, Hartford, Connecticut.
Architect, Edward Tuckerman
Potter. There are no Venetian
Gothic windows in Mark
Twain's house, but the powerful
polychromy bespeaks Ruskin's
teachings. Open to the public by
the Mark Twain Memorial.
Photo: Wayne Andrews.

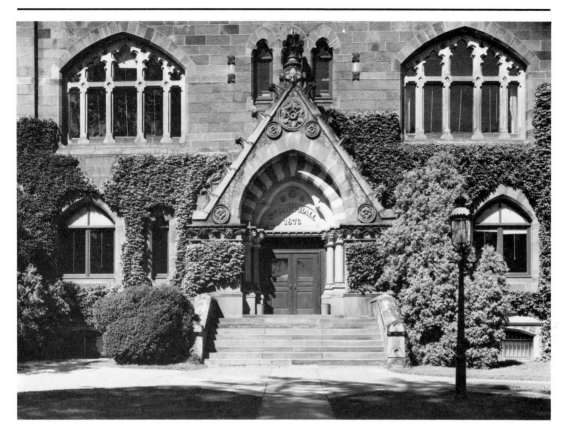

76
*Stuart Hall (1876), Princeton
University Seminary, Princeton,
New Jersey. Architect, William
Alexander Potter. Photo:
Wayne Andrews.*

77
Pennsylvania Academy of the
Fine Arts (1872–76),
Philadelphia, Pennsylvania.
Architects, Furness & Hewitt.
Photo: Wayne Andrews.
78
National Academy of Design
(1863), New York City;
demolished. Architect, Peter
Bonnett Wight. Photo: Museum
of the City of New York.

79
Battell Chapel (1876), Yale
University, New Haven,
Connecticut. Architect, Russell
Sturgis. Photo: Wayne Andrews.

style," Wright remembered in his autobiography. "His work had it too in spite of slipshod methods . . . a picturesque combination of gable, turret and hip with broad porches quietly domestic and gracefully picturesque. A contrast to the awkward stupidities and brutalities of the period, elsewhere."

The time has come to leave Ruskin, who did not enjoy a completely sane moment from 1888 until he died twelve years later. The cry of a peacock outside his window would distract him from the minerals he spent so much time classifying, bringing on not merely a nervous spasm but pure agony.

Ruskin's most faithful follower in England, William Morris, kept his sanity, demonstrating it for all to see on the day he retired from the board of directors of the copper mine that gave him his income. Seizing the top hat he was required to wear in the city, he sat down on it, squashing it forever out of shape. He was also fond of the children he fathered by his wife, the stable-keeper's daughter Jane Burden. Growing his hair long for their benefit, he would pull them up by having them cling to his beard.

Morris was a poet, as *the sick sure knowledge that things would never be the same* from his *Defence of Guinevere* would indicate, and he might have been an architect. In 1856, at twenty-two, he was apprenticed to George Edmund Street. But in 1859, when he began building the Red House at Bexley Heath outside of London, he left the execution of the plans to Philip Webb. He was tired, he said, of houses that were simply square boxes with lids, and the L-shaped dwelling he chose for his own home was an original work of art, no matter if its pointed windows recalled the Middle Ages. Whatever decoration there was, was constructional; no ornament could be said to have been applied.

He might have been a painter, like his friends in the Pre-Raphaelite movement, but he was destined to be the master propagandist for the revival of the arts and crafts. In 1861 he founded the firm of Morris, Marshall, Faulkner & Co. that specialized in everything from tapestries to tiles, and from stained-glass windows to wallpaper and furniture.

He had once considered taking holy orders while at Oxford, and there was a religious quality to his campaign for remaking interiors. "Have nothing in your houses that you do not know to be useful, or believe to be beautiful," he exhorted in a paragraph that Frank Lloyd Wright would appreciate. "I have never been in any rich man's house which would not have looked better for having a bonfire made outside of it of nine-tenths of all that it held," he warned his audience, preparing them for the news that he believed himself a Marxist. To Engels he was simply a "sentimental socialist." But then Engels, unlike Louis C. Tiffany in America, had no patience for a critic who cried, "I do not want art for a few."

There was no doubt he stood with Ruskin against the menace of restorations. "Architecture," he wrote, "long decaying, died out, as a popular art at least, just as the knowledge of mediaeval art was born. So that the civilized

80
Syracuse Savings Bank (1876),
Syracuse, New York. Architect,
James Lyman Silsbee. Photo:
Wayne Andrews.
81
The Red House (1860),
residence of William Morris,
Bexley Heath. Architects, Philip
Webb and William Morris. The
windows would have been
properly pointed or Gothic but
for the bricking in of the arches.
Photo: Wayne Andrews.

world of the nineteenth century has no style of its own amidst its wide knowledge of the styles of other centuries. From this lack and this gain arose in men's minds the strange idea of the restoration of ancient buildings; and a strange and most fatal idea, which by its very name implies that it is possible to strip from a building this, that and the other part of its history—of its life, that is—and then to stay the hand at some arbitrary point, and then leave it still historical, living and even as it once was."

Like Ruskin, he could discover nothing worth saving in the centuries that followed the "cataleptic sleep of the Renaissance." Far from admiring the cabinetmakers of the eighteenth century, he argued that "for us to set to work to imitate . . . the degraded and nightmare whims of the blasé and bankrupt aristocracy of Louis XV's time seems to me merely ridiculous. So I say our furniture should be good citizen's furniture, solid and wellmade and workmanlike and in design should have nothing about it that is not easily defensible, no monstrosities or extravagances, not even of beauty, lest we weary of it." Here was the perfect apology for the furniture that Gustav Stickley and Elbert Hubbard gave us in our grandfathers' generation, and it was not at all surprising that Hubbard, who revered, as Morris did not, all businessmen on their way to the top, set up a press in East Aurora, New York, in imitation of Morris's own Kelmscott Press.

"I believe," said Morris, "machines can do everything—except make works of art." Which was exactly what Frank Lloyd Wright was waiting to hear. For Morris was an individualist. He was also as irrational as Viollet-le-Duc, the great French Goth of the nineteenth century, was rational.

Eugène Emmanuel Viollet-le-Duc was twenty-four in 1838, when the government of Louis Philippe asked him to report on the Romanesque church of Vézelay for the Commission on Historic Monuments. He not only made the report but proceeded to restore Vézelay with a freedom that would have passed for impudence in the eyes of Ruskin and Morris. For all that, his talent as a restorer was triumphant. We owe him not only what passes for Vézelay and Notre Dame de Paris in our time, but also Pierrefonds, the medieval castle he remade for Napoleon III's son the Prince Imperial, and the present state of the city of Carcassonne. Even scholars may wonder whether the Carcassonne that was could be compared to what came about thanks to Viollet's theatrical imagination.

To Viollet the Renaissance may not have been an abomination from beginning to end, although he grew mortally tired of Palladio, Sansovino and Vignola during the seventeen months he spent as a student in Italy. What disgusted him was the influence of Louis XIV, who "succeeded, as regards art, in completely crushing the natural and original genius of the French people." He made this remark in his *Discourses on Architecture*, which happened to be translated in 1875 by Henry Van Brunt, an architect whose loyalty to Ruskin was evident in the Memorial Hall at Harvard which he and his partner,

82
Entrance to Carcassonne, as
restored c. 1852 by Eugène-
Emmanuel Viollet-le-Duc.
Photo: Wayne Andrews.

William R. Ware, built that very year.

The *Discourses* became a breviary to more than one generation of American architects. As for Viollet's *Dictionnaire Raisonné de l'Architecture,* it was no dictionary to Frank Lloyd Wright, but an inspiration, "the only really sensible book on architecture in the world." That book, he claimed, "was enough to keep one's faith in architecture in spite of architects."

"Every thrust of an arch found another thrust to cancel it," Viollet had written of the twelfth-century cathedrals in the *Discourses.* "Walls disappeared, and became only screens, not supports." Among those who could comprehend this saying in Chicago was Major William Le Baron Jenney, once an engineer on General Sherman's staff. Jenney was not an artist: Louis Sullivan thought he was a better gourmet than an architect. "The Major knew his vintages, every one, and his sauces, every one," said Sullivan. "He was also a master of the chafing dish and the charcoal *grille.*"

But Jenney seems to have been the first to translate Viollet's dictum into an actual skyscraper. The Home Insurance Company that he designed in 1883 for the southwest corner of La Salle and Adams streets is usually considered to be the *first* skyscraper—the first tall building to express its metal frame. It may not have been as handsome as Holabird & Roche's Tacoma Building nearby, which some scholars hold to be the first totally to express a steel frame, but both buildings—let us dismiss the argument for a minute—proved what the modern world could accomplish by exploiting, as did the master-builders of the cathedrals of the Middle Ages, the resources of engineering. With walls becoming screens, a revolution in the science of construction was inevitable.

Viollet was not the man to worry over being born in the century that witnessed the Home Insurance and the Tacoma. "Let men enjoy their inestimable privilege of grumbling over the degeneracy of our era as much as they will," he wrote, "but for me this century is as good as another, and I am willing to take it as it is." He was no antiquarian, no revivalist at heart. "If we would really have an architecture of the nineteenth century, we must, as a primary consideration, have a care that it is indeed our own," he argued, "taking its form and characteristics, not from precedent, but from ourselves. . . . A thing has style when it has the expression appropriate to its use."

Viollet could not have been too enthusiastic over Cass Gilbert's Woolworth Building in New York City, for its steel frame was masked by Gothic decoration which proved that the architect had the soul of an antiquarian. He should have been better pleased by Louis Sullivan's Guaranty Building in Buffalo, whose frame was enriched by decoration both pertinent and powerful. We say "should," because Viollet was too rational to go into ecstasy over the display of any man's genius. "If we get into the habit of proceeding by the light of reason," he advised, "if we erect a principle, the labor of composition is made possible, if not easy, for it follows an ordered, methodical march toward results which, if not masterpieces, are at least good, respectable works—and capable of possessing style."

To be respectable was not Sullivan's aim. He was there to create masterpieces that would honor Viollet's Gothic tradition, and perhaps he should be excused for indulging in a tirade when he came to consider the Chicago Fair of 1893 which was all too reminiscent of the invective of Ruskin. The Fair was an advertisement for the revival of the Renaissance. This was enough for Sullivan to decide that the whole show was " a naked exhibitionism of charlatanry in the higher feudal and domineering culture, conjoined with expert salesmanship of the materials of decay."

If Sullivan had been a wiser man, he might have understood that the tradition of the Gothic revival was too firmly fixed to be erased by the exhibits at the Fair. The Gothic was not even forgotten in the heyday of the Romanesque revival launched by Richardson. In 1885, when that desperately talented alcoholic Harvey Ellis was drawing the plans of the quite Richardsonian Grace Church that he and his brother were erecting in Scottsville, New York, he could not avoid recalling something like the tracery of the chapter house of Salisbury Cathedral when the time came to insert a trefoil above the entrance. Here was something that anticipated the fanciful Gothic in 1912 of Maybeck's Christian Science Church in Berkeley.

So much for outward and visible signs of the Gothic revival. There was no such sign in Sullivan's Guaranty Building, so completely was the Gothic tradition assimilated. Nor was there a single crocket or finial to be found in the Low house of 1887 at Bristol, Rhode Island, the greatest of all the achievements of McKim, Mead & White in their shingle style. Yet this was, in its way, a Gothic creation. Its shingles testified that McKim comprehended, as perfectly as Downing could have desired, the necessity for expressing the nature of materials. And it was even more a part of its site than any castle on the Hudson.

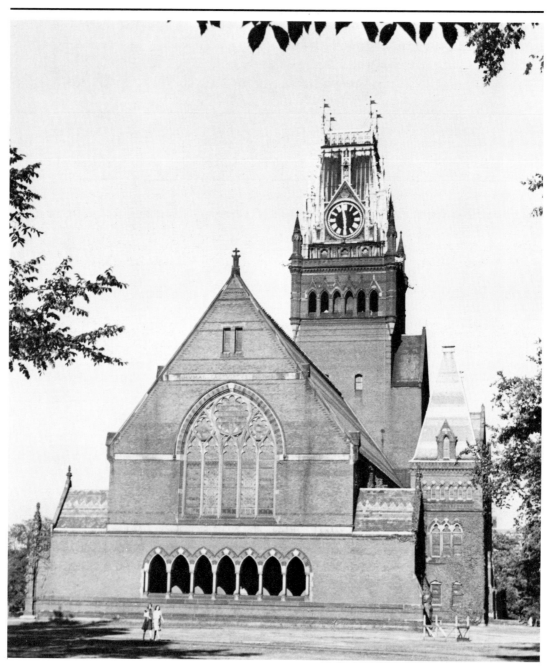

83
Memorial Hall (1875),
Harvard University,
Cambridge, Massachusetts.
Architects, Ware & Van Brunt.
The tower has since been
removed. Photo:
Wayne Andrews.

84
Residence (1887) of William G.
Low, Bristol, Rhode Island.
Architects, McKim, Mead &
White. Although almost any
architect would agree that this
was one of the great houses of the
world in the nineteenth century,
it was recently demolished. The
new owner of the property, for
reasons which are not clear,
decided that it was not
sufficiently "modern." Photo:
Wayne Andrews.

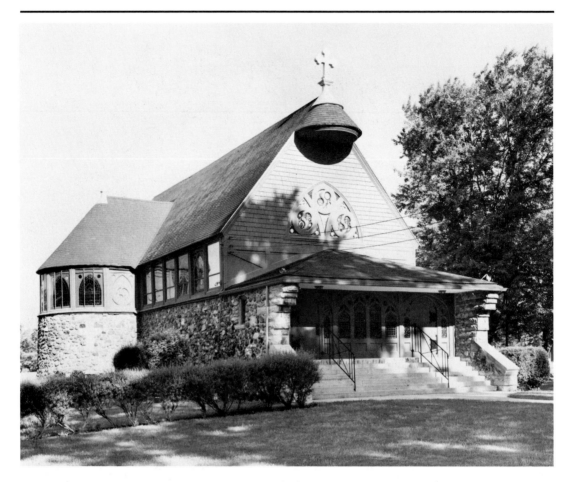

85
Grace Church (1885),
Scottsville, New York. Architects,
Harvey & Charles Ellis. Photo:
Wayne Andrews.
86
Guaranty Building (1895),
Buffalo, New York. Architects,
Adler & Sullivan. Photo:
Wayne Andrews.

87
Home Insurance Building
(1883–85), Chicago, Illinois;
demolished. Architect, William
LeBaron Jenney. Originally
nine stories high; two extra
stories added in 1890. Although
a portion of the total load was
carried on granite piers, this
building gave the world an
idea of what might happen if
walls became screens instead of
supports. Photo: Chicago
Architectural
Photographing Co.

88
Detail, First Church of Christ
Scientist (1912), Berkeley,
California. Architect, Bernard
Maybeck. Photo:
Wayne Andrews.

Gothic
Dusk

Now that everything has come so neatly into focus, and the masters of the Gothic revival stand revealed as the prophets of modern architecture, we can no longer avoid mentioning Ralph Adams Cram, a Goth who had no patience whatever with "the modernist idea" in the field of art. "It has its place," said Cram, "and it may and should go to it. Its boundaries are definite and fixed, and beyond them it cannot go, for the Angel of Decency, Propriety and Reason stands there with a flaming sword."

To Cram, the steel frame that Sullivan endowed with such grace was a living lie. "We do, indeed, indulge in skeleton construction and reinforced concrete and other structural expedients and substitutes, but deep in our racial consciousness, as in that of all other Anglo-Saxon peoples, is the solid conviction that, after all, there are but three real things in the world — the home, the school and the Church — and when we are dealing with eternal verities, honest and enduring construction is alone advisable." As for skyscrapers, Cram was sure, even in 1936, that "they are already becoming slightly *vieux jeu*, except in the smaller cities of the Middle West, where they have no excuse at all."

Like Frank Lloyd Wright, Cram was the son of a Unitarian minister, but there all similarity ended. He was to find his haven in the Anglo-Catholic wing of the Episcopal Church, to which he was to be remarkably faithful, perhaps too faithful for Anglo-Catholics with a sense of humor. For Cram could be loyal — too loyal, for example, to King Charles I, whom he referred to as Charles the Martyr. Another favorite of his was Benito Mussolini, whose corporate state he announced in 1937 was "the only sane and logical system now in process." He did approve of Franklin D. Roosevelt, but only because he was imposing a "mediaeval system" on the United States.

Although he consented to become chairman of the Department of Architecture at MIT in 1914, he never believed for a second that his mission was to help young men get ahead. "I took the position at Technology," he admitted, "that my function was not to get men into the architectural profession, but to keep them out." Cram's students were informed that Thomas Jefferson was no better than a dilettante, and that the Gothic of the age of Downing could not be discussed if women were present.

"Prior to 1830 nothing really bad had been done," he revealed in his autobiography. "From then on, nothing good, except sporadically, came into existence, and for fifty years architecture in America fell to a lower level than history had ever before recorded." We were then experiencing what Cram referred to as "Carpenter's Gothic," and on this subject he would admit no argument. "The sheer savagery of those boxlike wooden structures, with their toothpick pinnacles, their adventitious buttresses of seven-eighths-inch board, find no rival in all history."

Cram eventually received his fair share of honorary degrees. These he was careful to list on the title pages of his books. He intended that the world

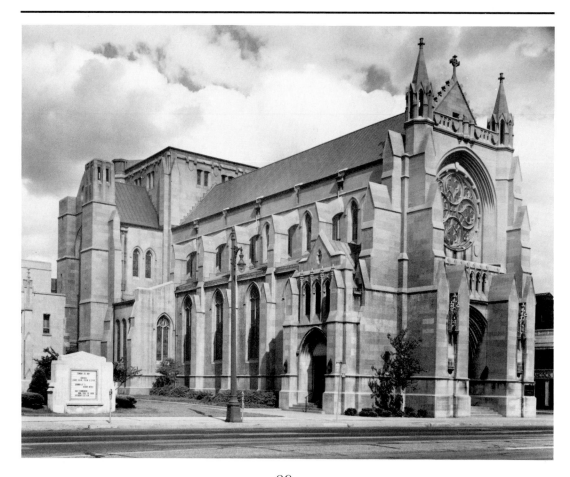

89
St. Paul's Cathedral (1908 –
11), Detroit, Michigan.
Architect, Ralph Adams Cram.
The church lacks the tower for
which Cram pleaded. Photo:
Wayne Andrews.

should listen to his message, which an unfriendly critic might take to be the notion that the painstaking reproduction of medieval trappings was infinitely preferable to any invention. As he himself said, "The obvious inference was that the thing for me was to take up English Gothic at the point where it was cut off during the reign of Henry VIII and go on from that point, developing the style England had made her own, and along what might be assumed to be logical lines, with due regard for the changing conditions of contemporary culture."

What all this meant was made visible at West Point, at Princeton, where he labored over the graduate school, and in Detroit, where he was responsible in 1908–11 for St. Paul's Cathedral. At St. Paul's there is no hint of the "aerial masses" that Horace Walpole so loved. In fact, the stone piers of the nave are so far from soaring that their principal function may be said to mask the altar from the view of the congregation.

Cram has nowhere left us his impressions of Antonio Gaudí's Cathedral of the Holy Family in Barcelona, but it is easy to imagine his embarassment in the presence of the sculpted forms of the Catalan master of the Gothic revival. Nor did Cram live to inspect Eero Saarinen's TWA terminal at Kennedy, another example of architecture as sculpture that could scarcely have been invented but for the Gothic precedent in Barcelona. But we may easily conceive of Cram's anger had he seen Auldbrass Plantation at Yemassee, South Carolina, where Frank Lloyd Wright in 1940 paid his respects to the Carpenter's Gothic that Cram found so horrid. The brackets beneath the eaves of Auldbrass might almost have been planned by the artisan who sawed the jigsaw detail of the James Lenox gate lodge at New Hamburg, New York, a hundred years before.

In 1975 the time for tantrums a la Cram has passed. The tradition of the Gothic revival has been so perfectly assimilated, and the triumph of modern architecture so complete—perhaps too complete, for there is such a thing as self-satisfaction—that generosity has come into fashion, generosity to the followers of the Renaissance tradition that Ruskin and the others so despised.

The adventures of the Gothic revival may never come to an end, but an end of some sort was provided on October 28, 1963, when the widow of Eero Saarinen joined Philip Johnson, Mies van der Rohe's associate in the Seagram Building, to protest in a picket line the demolition of Pennsylvania Station in New York City. This Roman monument was one of the principal achievements of Charles Follen McKim, who had done so much to promote the cause of the Renaissance in the United States, but it was nonetheless recognized as a great monument. This would have been unthinkable thirty years before, when prigs teaching architectural history could not spew enough venom in McKim's direction.

The time had come to render justice to a fallen foe. The Renaissance itself might have something to offer in the years ahead.

90
Auldbrass Plantation (1940),
residence of Leigh Stevens,
Yemassee, South Carolina.
Architect, Frank Lloyd Wright.
Photo: Wayne Andrews.
91
Apartment house (1951), 860
Lake Shore Drive, Chicago,
Illinois. Architect, Ludwig Miës
van der Rohe. Miës, who spent
his life developing a formula for
glass towers, might have been
just the man to please Viollet-le-
Duc. In heavier hands than
those of Miës the formula can
become a bore. But here is a
preeminent example of walls
becoming screens, not supports.
Photo: Wayne Andrews.

92
Cathedral of the Holy Family
(1884–1926), Barcelona.
Architect, Antonio Gaudí.
Photo: Wayne Andrews.
93
Interior of TWA Terminal
(1962), Kennedy Airport, New
York City. Architects, Eero
Saarinen Associates. Photo:
Wayne Andrews.

Acknowledgments

I am indebted to Avery Library, Columbia University, for the use of photographs of two views of Fonthill Abbey from Rutter's Delineations of Fonthill; to the Chicago Architectural Photographing Company for the Home Insurance Building; to the Metropolitan Museum for the elevations and plan of Glen Ellen as well as the plan of the Harral house; to the Museum of the City of New York for the National Academy of Design; to the National Portrait Gallery, London, for George Dance's drawing of Horace Walpole; to the New-York Historical Society for Birch's view of Sedgley and Morse's Allegorical Landscape; to Rockefeller Center for St. Patrick's Cathedral; and to Nemo Warr for photographing Downing's house as reproduced in Downing's Treatise. All other photographs are my own — with a special word of thanks to Dick Schuler, Ernest Pile and their associates at Compo Photocolor who have developed my film, enlarged my negatives and given me so much good advice for so many years.

For permission to quote, I am indebted to Yale University Press for passages from W. S. Lewis's edition of the Correspondence of Horace Walpole (New Haven, Conn., 1937–75).

Finally, I am thankful that my manuscript was read by my good friends Alan Burnham, Larry Curry, Leonard K. Eaton, Goldwin Smith and Christopher Tunnard.

Bibliography

Alexander, Boyd, ed., *The Journal of William Beckford in Portugal and Spain*, New York, 1955

Andrews, Wayne, "Alexander Jackson Davis," *Architectural Review*, May 1951

———, "America's Gothic Hour," *Town and Country*, November 1947

———, *Architecture, Ambition and Americans*, New York, 1955

Ball, Jean, *Historic Buildings in Warren County*, Warren, Pa., 1971

Brown, Roscoe C. E., *Church of the Holy Trinity*, New York, 1922

Chapman, Guy, *Beckford*, London, 1940

———, ed., Travel Diaries of William Beckford, 2 vols., Cambridge, 1928

———, ed., *William Beckford's Vathek*, 2 vols., Cambridge, 1929

Clark, Sir Kenneth, *The Gothic Revival: An Essay in the History of Taste*, London, 1928

Clark, Robert Judson, ed., *The Arts and Crafts Movement in America 1887–1916*, Princeton, 1972

Condit, Carl W., *The Chicago School of Architecture*. Chicago, 1964.

Conover, Jewel Helen, *Nineteenth-Century Houses in Western New York*, Albany, 1966

Cram, Ralph Adams, *My Life in Architecture*, Boston, 1936

———, *The Ministry of Art*, Freeport, 1967

Crook, J. Mordaunt, "Strawberry Hill Revisited," *Country Life*, June 7, 14 and 21, 1973

———, et al., eds., *The Correspondence of Horace Walpole*, 39 vols. to date, New Haven, 1937–73

Demetz, Frédéric-Auguste and Blouet, Guillaume, *Rapports sur les Pénitenciers des Etats-Unis*, Paris, 1837

Dobson, Austin, *Horace Walpole: A Memoir*, London, 1927

Downing, Andrew Jackson, *Cottage Residences*, New York, 1847

———, *Rural Essays*, New York, 1853

———, *A Treatise on the Theory and Practice of Landscape Gardening*, New York, 1860

Evans, Joan, *John Ruskin*, London, 1954

Ferrey, Benjamin, *Recollections of Augustus Northmore Welby Pugin and of His Father*, London, 1861

Fothergill, Brian, *Sir William Hamilton: Envoy Extraordinary*, New York, 1969

Gebhard, David, et al., *A Guide to Architecture in San Francisco and Northern California*, Santa Barbara, Calif., 1973

———, *A Guide to Architecture in Southern California*, Los Angeles, 1965

Greif, Constance, et al., *Princeton Architecture*, Princeton, 1967

Henderson, Philip, *William Morris*, London, 1967

James, Admiral Sir William, *John Ruskin and Effie Gray*, New York, 1947

Ketton-Cremer, R. W., *Horace Walpole: A Biography*, London, 1940

Kirker, Harold, *California's Architectural Frontier*, San Marino, Calif., 1960

Lancaster, Clay, *Back Streets and Pine Trees: The Work of John McMurtry*, Lexington, 1956

Landy, Jacob, *The Architecture of Minard Lafever*, New York, 1970

Leon, Derrick, *Ruskin, The Great Victorian*, London, 1949

Lewis, Wilmarth S., "The Genesis of Strawberry Hill," *Metropolitan Museum Studies*, 1934

———, *Horace Walpole*, Washington, 1960

———, et al., eds., *The Correspondence of Horace Walpole*, 39 vols. to date, New Haven, 1937–75

Mackail, J. W., *The Life of William Morris*, London, 1950

Malo, Paul, *Landmarks of Rochester and Monroe County*, Syracuse, N. Y., 1969

McKee, Harley J., *Architecture Worth Saving in Onondaga County*, Syracuse, N. Y., 1964

Nevins, Allan, ed., *The Diary of Philip Hone*, New York, 1936

Newcomb, Rexford, *Architecture in Old Kentucky*, Urbana, Ill., 1953

Norton, Sarah and Howe, Mark A. De Wolfe, eds., *Letters of Charles Eliot Norton*, 2 vols., Boston, 1913

O'Gorman, James F., *The Architecture of Frank Furness*, Philadelphia, 1973

Oliver, J. W., *The Life of William Beckford*, London, 1932

Peat, Wilbur D., *Indiana Houses of the Nineteenth Century*, Indianapolis, 1962

Pugin, A. W. N., *An Apology for the Revival of Christian Architecture*, London, 1843

———, *Contrasts*, Salisbury, 1836

———, *The True Principles of Pointed or Christian Architecture*, London, 1841

Ruskin, John, *Letters to Charles Eliot Norton*, 2 vols., Boston, 1904

———, *Praeterita*, London, 1949

———, *The Seven Lamps of Architecture*, London, 1940

———, *The Stones of Venice*, 3 vols., London, 1935

Scully, Arthur, Jr., *James Dakin: Architect*, Baton Rouge, La., 1973

Smith, J. Frazier, *White Pillars*, New York, 1941

Stanton, Phoebe, *The Gothic Revival and American Church Architecture*, Baltimore, 1968

———, *Pugin*, London, 1972

Stewart, William R., *Grace Church and Old New York*, New York, 1924

Sullivan, Louis H., *The Autobiography of an Idea*, New York, 1924

Summerson, John, *Heavenly Mansions*, New York, n. d.

Teeters, Negley K., "The Early Days of the Eastern State Penitentiary," *Pennsylvania History*, October 1949

Trappes-Lomax, Michael, *Pugin*, London, 1933

Upjohn, Everard M., *Richard Upjohn: Architect and Churchman*, New York, 1939

Upjohn, Richard, *Upjohn's Rural Architecture*, New York, 1852

Vanderbilt, Kermit, *Charles Eliot Norton*, Cambridge, 1959

Viollet-le-Duc, Eugène Emmanuel, *Discourses on Architecture* (translated by Henry Van Brunt), Boston, 1875

Wight, Peter Bonnett, "Reminiscences of Russell Sturgis," *Architectural Record*, August, 1909

Wightwick, George, *Hints to Young Architects (with Additional Notes by A. J. Downing)*, New York, 1847

Wright, Frank Lloyd, *An Autobiography*, New York, 1932

Index

About the Author
Wayne Andrews is currently the Archives
of American Art Professor at Wayne State University
in Detroit. He is the author of six books on architecture
(Architecture, Ambition, and Americans,
Architecture in America, Architecture in Michigan,
Architecture in Chicago and Mid-America,
Architecture in New York and Architecture in New England),
as well as four social histories (The Vanderbilt Legend,
Battle for Chicago, Germaine: A Portrait of Madame de Staël
and Siegfried's Curse: The German
Journey From Nietzsche to Hesse).